KIDS EXPERIENCING GOD AT HOME

KIM BLACKABY & RICK OSBORNE

LifeWay Press®
Nashville, TN 37234

Published by LifeWay Press®

© 2013 Kim Blackaby and Rick Osborne

No part of this book may be reproduced or transmitted in any form or by any means, electronic or mechanical, including photocopying and recording, or by any information storage or retrieval system, except as may be expressly permitted in writing by the publisher. Requests for permission should be addressed in writing to LifeWay Press®; One LifeWay Plaza; Nashville, TN 37234.

ISBN 9781415877357
Item 005558320

Dewey decimal classification: 649
Subject headings: PARENTING \ CHILD REARING \ GOD

To order additional copies of this resource, write to LifeWay Church Resources Customer Service; One LifeWay Plaza; Nashville, TN 37234-0113; fax (615) 251-5933; phone toll free (800) 458-2772; order online at *www.lifeway.com*; e-mail orderentry@lifeway.com; or visit the LifeWay Christian Store serving you.

Printed in the United States of America

Kids Ministry Publishing
LifeWay Church Resources
One LifeWay Plaza
Nashville, TN 37234-0172

Table of Contents

Welcome to the Adventure!.. 5
Using the *Experiencing God* Resources.. 7
Suggested Schedule.. 8
Preparing Myself.. 9

SESSION 1: The Adventure Begins.. 10

SESSION 2: God Is at Work... 18

SESSION 3: God Loves Me.. 26

SESSION 4: God Wants Me to Be a Part of His Work........................ 34

SESSION 5: God Speaks, I Listen.. 42

SESSION 6: I Must Have Faith.. 50

SESSION 7: Adjusting To God's Plan.. 58

SESSION 8: Experiencing God.. 68

SESSION 9: The Choice Is Mine.. 78

Handouts.. 88
Reality Posters..Insert

WHEN WAS THE LAST TIME
YOU EXPERIENCED GOD WORKING
IN YOUR LIFE?

Welcome to the adventure!

We hope that as you lead children to understand the concepts of *Experiencing God*, you, too, will experience Him in new ways. In addition, we hope you will experience the adventure of walking with Him and seeing Him work through you to accomplish His kingdom purposes in the world.

Before beginning to lead the children to experience this material, we recommend you read and study *Experiencing God: Knowing and Doing the Will of God* by Henry Blackaby and Claude V. King. Be sure you have a good understanding of the seven realities outlined in *Experiencing God*.

- **Reality 1:** God is always at work on mission to redeem a lost world. Your job is to be aware of where He is at work.

- **Reality 2:** God pursues a continuing love relationship with you that is real and personal.

- **Reality 3:** God invites you to become involved with Him in His work.

- **Reality 4:** God speaks by the Holy Spirit through the Bible, prayer, circumstances, and the church to reveal Himself, His purposes, and His ways.

- **Reality 5:** God's invitation for you to work with Him always leads you to a crisis of belief that requires faith and action. A "Crisis of Belief" is not a crisis in your circumstances necessarily, but a spiritual point of decision in which you must decide what you believe about God and act on that belief.

- **Reality 6:** You must make major adjustments in your life to join God in what He is doing.

- **Reality 7:** You come to know God by experience as you obey Him, and He accomplishes His work through you.

Our desire is to present these realities to children to help them see that God is at work in their lives as well. For this reason, we have selected Bible passages that focus on children and young people. Experiencing God is not just something that happens to adults or through great dramatic displays of His power. Experiencing God is a daily adventure of learning to walk with Him, recognize when He is speaking, and where He is working in our world. Kids too, can be a part of this adventure.

Kim Blackaby and Rick Osborne

> GOD, HELP ME EXPERIENCE YOU AS I GUIDE CHILDREN TO EXPERIENCE YOU.

Using the Experiencing God Resources

Working with children is an adventure. Guiding children to experience what God is doing in and through their lives is a privilege and calling. Over the next nine weeks, you have the opportunity to help children explore truths related to knowing and doing God's will.

The materials are designed to be led by one adult as other adults participate with a small group of children. Take time to get to know each child individually and be willing to assist as needed in completing the activities.

Each session is designed to last 60 to 75 minutes (see page 8 for scheduling options). Some of the activities will require more time than others. You may need to adjust the amount of time for the activities.

The *Experiencing God at Home Leader Guide* provides you with step-by-step directions on leading each session. Spend time reading and reflecting on the information in the "Teacher Preparation" section. Read, study, and apply the biblical content to your life before guiding children to read, study, and apply the material to their lives.

Each session will begin with a "Getting Ready" activity. This activity will guide the children to use their decoders to "Crack the Code" for the session. This code is related to the life application or reality being studied during the session. Guide each child to begin the "Getting Ready" activity as she enters the room. The kids' learner booklets will be used during the session. Following "Getting Ready" is a time of "Excite." These activities are designed to create excitement and build energy as you begin the large group time. The "Examine" time is to introduce the Bible story, Bible truth, life application, or the key verse for the session. Most "Examine" activities are designed to be completed in 10 minutes. The main part of the session is "Explore." In "Explore," the children will explore the biblical content and discover how individuals experienced God. The children will be challenged to explore how God is working in their lives as well. In "Engage," the children will be provided three options. You may choose to allow all the children to complete the same activity, or provide all three and allow the children to choose which activities they wish to participate in. Each activity is designed to last 20 minutes. If you need additional time, allow the children to complete one activity, and then select another. The final aspect of each session is "Ending the Session." This is a wrap-up, review time of the Bible story, key Bible verse, and life application.

Each week the children will receive an *Experiencing God Kids Learner Booklet*. Nine different booklets are included in each package. Separate the books and keep them together until the appropriate session. Call attention to the "Experiencing God at Home" activities on page 12 of each booklet. Challenge the children to complete the activities with their families during the week.

Ready to begin? Read the "Preparing Myself" materials on page 9. Take time to pray for God's guidance before beginning to prepare each session. Ask God to help you experience Him working in and through you as you lead the sessions.

Suggested Schedule

	60 minutes	75 minutes	90 minutes
Getting Ready	*Begin as soon as the first child arrives*		
Excite	5	5	10
Examine	8	10	10
Explore	25	25	25
Engage	20	30	40
Ending the Session	3	5	5

- The *Experiencing God* resources are designed for 60-75 minutes.

- If additional time is needed, allow the children to participate in more than one "Engage" activity.

Preparing Myself

Review the seven realities of *Experiencing God* (page 5). What do these statements mean to you? How have you seen these realities played out in your life? Read the realities as they will be presented to children. Reflect on the questions.

- **Reality 1: God is always at work around me.** When was the last time you observed God working around you? What did He do?

- **Reality 2: God wants a personal relationship with me.** When did God invite you to a love relationship with Him? How did God pursue you?

- **Reality 3: God wants me to be a part of His work.** How and when has God invited you to join Him in His work? Perhaps your decision to lead this study was a response to His invitation to be involved in what He is doing in the children's lives.

- **Reality 4: God speaks and shows me what He wants me to do.** How has God spoken to you through His Word, prayer, circumstances, or the body of Christ? How do you feel about what He revealed?

- **Reality 5: I must have faith and take action to follow God and join in His work.** Do you have faith and take action to follow God or stand back and watch things happen? How would your life be different if you immediately joined God in His work?

- **Reality 6: I must be willing to make changes in my life to follow God's plan.** What adjustments have you made in your life, schedule, priorities, and daily choices to join God in His work?

- **Reality 7: I know and experience God when I obey Him.** How have you experienced God as you stepped out in obedience to Him? How have you come to know Him better? What did you learn about God when you obeyed Him?

Be prepared to share with the children how you experience God working in your life. Include facts related to when you became a Christian, what God is currently doing in your life, or a particular Scripture that has spoken to you.

LEADER GUIDE PREPARING MYSELF

Session 1: THE ADVENTURE BEGINS

Teacher Preparation

BIBLE PASSAGE
John 5:17,19-24

BIBLE TRUTH
When we enter into a relationship with God, He invites us to an adventure in which we can be part of His work and experience Him in amazing ways.

LIFE APPLICATION
I can know God and be a part of the adventure of working with Him.

KEY VERSE
Jeremiah 29:13

PRAYER CHALLENGE
Before beginning your planning, pray God will prepare your heart and work through you to speak to the children. Pray God will prepare the children to hear and apply what they learn so they can experience all He has planned for them.

- Read John 5:16-30. These verses express the heart of *Experiencing God*. Through these verses we see the seven realities modeled by Jesus Himself. Jesus stated that God is always at work—He had plans and purposes He wanted to accomplish. Jesus joined the Father in His work—participating in what God was already doing.
- Reflect on Jesus' words. God had revealed to Jesus what He was doing as well as His plans and purposes. Jesus had spent time alone with His Father. Jesus knew God's voice, He heard from Him, and He acted and taught only as the Father directed Him. Do you know God's voice? How do you react when He reveals His plans to you?
- Place yourself at the scene described in John 5:16-30. Jesus walked in dependence with His Father. He stated He could do nothing by Himself.
- Read "Preparing Myself" (page 9). Compare and contrast your obedience, dedication, and commitment to Jesus'.
- Respond to this question, "How is God at work in my life?" Throughout the study take time to help the children understand God is at work in your life. Share personal experiences and relate the studies to your life.
- Think about the children in your ministry. How is God at work in their lives? Is God working in their lives the way He worked in Tom and Kim Blackaby's family? For several years Tom, Kim, and their children lived in Norway. Their children attended an international school where, because of work or military connections, children were always coming and going. The Blackabys helped their children see how God could use them as they befriended new students. The kids learned by reaching out to the new students, they could be a part of God's work.
- Think of your favorite Bible person (other than Jesus). Why do you admire this person? How did this individual experience God in his life? What did God do through him? In what ways are you like the person?
- Answer these questions: what do you want God to do through you? Are you willing to allow God to work through you? What changes do you need to make in your life for Him to work through you? Are you willing to make these changes? Why or why not?
- Spend time alone with God. During your quiet time, ask God to help you experience Him in ways you have never done before.

- Reread page 9. Pray through each statement. Ask God to help you communicate the importance of each statement to the children. Invite God to work through you, helping you model each of the realities.

Getting Ready

- Welcome each child.
- Distribute *Experiencing God Kids Learner Guide* and pencils.
- Guide the children to complete "Crack the Code" (page 1).
- Say: "Today we will discover how God is working in our lives."

Excite (5-8 MINUTES)

- Distribute markers and crayons.
- Guide the children to complete "An Experience with God" (page 2).
- Talk about your favorite Bible person as the children complete the activity.
- Invite the children to show their pictures and tell about their favorite Bible times persons.
- Ask: "Why is this your favorite Bible times person? What amazing things did God do through the person you drew? What did he learn about God through the person's experiences?"

Examine (10 MINUTES)

- State: "Today we will discover how some people in the Bible experienced God as well as how we can experience Him in our lives. God is real and wants to work in our lives just as He worked in the lives of people in the Bible."
- Say: "God worked through these people to do amazing things. These people had adventures with God, and not only learned about Him, they allowed God to work in their lives."
- Ask: "Are you willing for God to work in your life? How would you feel if He did something amazing through you? Would you be surprised? Would you be scared? How would people around you respond?"
- Allow the children to respond to the questions.
- Invite a volunteer to read aloud the "Crack the Code" message.
- Display "Reality 1-7" posters.
- Invite volunteers to read aloud the posters.
- Say: "Over the next eight weeks, we will learn about these realities of experiencing God. In today's study, we will learn how God wants to use us. He loves us and wants us to be involved in some adventures with Him."
- Display the mirror.
- Move the mirror in front of the children's faces so they can see their reflections.

SUPPLIES AND PREP
Bibles, Session 1 of *Experiencing God Kids Learner Guide* (1 per child), markers, crayons, tape, hand-held mirror, construction paper, pencils, "Reality 1-7" posters (Insert), scissors, brad

- Write the words of Jeremiah 29:13 on the construction paper. Display.

CRACK THE CODE
I will learn how God is working in my life.

TIP
Provide additional mirrors if you have a large group of children.

LEADER GUIDE **SESSION 1**

- Ask: "What is the purpose of a mirror?"
- Discuss responses.
- State: "Show me how you look when you are happy. How do you look when you are sad? Upset? Scared? Mad?"
- Show the children their reflections.
- Comment on the children's facial expressions.
- Say: "Our expressions tell how we are feeling. Let's make some facial expressions during our Bible story. Listen as I read aloud the Bible story Scripture and think about how the people felt. After I read the story, I will retell it, pausing for you to show me facial expressions."

Explore (25 MINUTES)

TIP
Assist children in locating Bible passages.

BIBLE STORY
- Guide the children to locate John 5 in their Bibles.
- Read aloud John 5:17,19-24.
- Ask: "By whose authority did Jesus say He was able to perform miracles?"
- Continue: "Let me retell the story, adding in some details that are not recorded in these specific verses. This time, show me how you would feel during these events."
- Retell the Bible story, pausing as indicated for facial expressions.

TIP
Practice telling the Bible story several times. Include inflections in your voice, appropriate body language, and seek to communicate the emotions of the individuals.

THE FATHER AND THE SON

Jesus and His followers were in the city of Jerusalem for a special feast. Jesus had taught and healed many people. *[Pause.]* People who had been blind were now able to see. *[Pause.]* People who could not walk were able to walk. *[Pause.]* People who were very sick and in pain were healed and made healthy. *[Pause.]* Word spread that Someone who could do miracles was in Jerusalem. Many people searched for Jesus. *[Pause.]*

The people listened as Jesus taught. *[Pause.]* He was a great teacher! He explained the Scriptures in ways the people had never heard before. He used a lot of stories and illustrations that made the people think about God and His commands. *[Pause.]*

The Jewish leaders and priests did not like what Jesus taught. *[Pause.]* The priests had been to school with the rabbis (religious teachers) and they thought they were the only ones who knew how to correctly teach the people. The Jewish leaders and priests did not like the attention Jesus was getting and the miracles He was performing. *[Pause.]* Jesus even healed people on the Sabbath! *[Pause.]* A Jewish person knew he was not supposed to do any work on the Sabbath day.

Jesus knew the Jewish leaders were upset with Him. *[Pause.]* These men wanted to know from whom He received the right to teach and heal people. Jesus told the people that His Father, God, was the One who told Him what to do and teach, and gave Him the power to perform miracles. God was always working in the world. Jesus was simply doing what God wanted. *[Pause.]* Jesus was God's Son, but He could not do anything on His own. Jesus received His power from God. Jesus looked to see what God was doing and joined God in His actions. Jesus showed God's love to the people. He spent time alone communicating (praying) with God. Jesus listened to and obeyed God. God did amazing things through Jesus. *[Pause.]*

- Say: "The most amazing thing Jesus did was die on a cross for our sins. *[Pause.]* Jesus did this to show how much God loves us and to make a way for us to have a relationship with God. Jesus wants us to be a part of the adventure of working with God to accomplish His purpose in this world. *[Pause.]* When we follow Jesus' example of trusting and obeying God, He will work through us, too." *[Pause.]*
- Review: "What amazing things did God do through Jesus? From whom did Jesus say He received the power to do these things? How did the people respond to Jesus? Why did the religious leaders not like what Jesus was doing? How do you think you would have responded if you had been in Jerusalem during this time? How does it make you feel to know God wants to do amazing things through you?"
- Guide the children to locate Jeremiah 29:13 in their Bibles.
- Select a volunteer to read aloud the verse.
- Call attention to the verse poster.
- Invite the group to read aloud the verse.
- Guide the children to complete "A Verse to Remember" (page 5).
- Ask: "What does it mean to seek God? In what ways can we seek Him? Will we find God when we seek Him? How do we know this to be true?"
- Explain: "God wants us to seek Him and His will (His plans) for our lives. Sometimes when we hear the word *seek*, we may think something is lost or hidden and we have to search to find it. God is not hiding from us. He is everywhere! When we ask God to show us His plan for our lives, He will. He will use us to do amazing things if we are willing to trust and obey Him."
- Ask: "If you could be any person in the Bible, other than Jesus, who would you like to be? Why?"
- Invite the kids to share their responses.
- Say: "Not everyone in the Bible experienced God in the same way. Open your booklets to 'How They Experienced God' (page 4). Match the person's name with the way he experienced God."
- Pause as the children complete the activity.
- Reveal the answers. Talk about the ways these people experienced God.
- Invite the children to locate "It's So Amazing to Experience God" (pages 6-7).
- Direct the children to work through the maze.
- Discuss the actions and how they can help the children experience God.

A VERSE TO REMEMBER
Seek, God, Heart

HOW THEY EXPERIENCED GOD
Abraham/Sarah—baby
Moses—burning bush
Samuel—"Samuel"
Noah—ark
Elijah—altar
Mary—"You will have ..."
Paul—bright light
Peter—chains falling off

LEADER GUIDE SESSION 1

- Continue: "Jesus is our example of living in ways that God wants. Every day we should seek God as Jesus did and live in ways that are a part of His plan and work. Think back to the Bible story. In what ways did Jesus follow God's plan? What were some things God did through Jesus?"
- Share how you experience God working in your life. Include information based on being a part of God's work in the world, how God speaks to you, how you have seen God working, and what you learned about God.
- Guide the children to complete "What I Want to Happen in My Life" (page 3).
- Invite the children to share what they hope God will do in their lives.
- Ask: "Do you think you are too young for God to use?"
- Continue: "No one is too young, too old, too short, too tall, too anything for God to use. In our study, we will learn how God can use anyone who is willing."
- Direct the children to bow their heads.
- Pray, thanking God for His love for each person and for sending Jesus to show how we can know God and be a part of His work. Ask God to help each person seek and know Him better. Thank Him for His wonderful plan He has for each person.

TIP
Have extra time? Read aloud the first "What God Did" story ("Tricia's Story", page 8). Talk about Tricia's choices and how her decisions impacted herself and Tracy.

Engage (20 MINUTES)

SUPPLIES AND PREP
Scissors
- Copy and cut apart "Prayer and Solution" (Insert). (Keep matching sets together.)

TIP
Correct "Prayer and Solution" matches are listed on page 17.

ENGAGE OPTION ONE: GOD HEARS AND ANSWERS PRAYERS
- Ask: "What is prayer?"
- Continue: "*Prayer* is 'communicating with God'. When we pray, we not only talk to God, we listen to Him. Let's play a game to help us learn about prayer and how God can help us."
- Distribute "Prayer and Solution" cards (1 per child).
- Explain: "Some of you have an example of someone asking for God's help. The others have answers to the prayers. Move around the room and locate the person with the card that matches yours. When you think you found the matching cards, bring them to me. I will tell you if the cards match."
- Allow the children to match the cards and verify the matches.
- Guide the children back to their seats.
- Read aloud each set of cards, discussing the information.
- Ask: "Do you think Jesus communicated with God? How about other people in the Bible, did they pray to God? How important was prayer to them? How important is prayer to us?"
- Say: "As we learn to experience God, we will learn why it is important to communicate with God. What do we call communicating with God? *(prayer)* We can pray about anything, anywhere, and at any time. We can know God will hear and answer our prayers in His time and in His way."
- Invite the children to share prayer requests.
- Pray for each child by name. Ask God to help each individual experience Him.

EXPERIENCING GOD AT HOME **KIDS**

ENGAGE OPTION TWO: TREASURE HUNT

- Guide the children to the center of the room.
- Explain: "Today we're on a treasure hunt. I hid a small box somewhere in the room. Your task is to locate the box, but do not let anyone else know you located it. When you find the box, do not touch it, or tell anyone where it is hidden. Come whisper to me where the box is located. If you are correct, I will give you a prize."
- Guide each child to locate the box, whisper the location, and receive a prize.
- Re-hide the box and play again as time permits.
- Gather the children together.
- Ask: "Did I hide the box for you to find, or did I not want you to find it?'"
- Invite the children to respond.
- Explain: "I hid the box for you to find. I was not trying to keep the box from you. If I had wanted to keep you from finding the box, I would have hidden it in a more difficult place or not brought it to church at all."
- Ask: "Did you receive a prize when you found the box, or did I keep the prize away from you?"
- Explain: "To receive a prize, you had to find the box. The purpose of our game was for me to hide the box, each of you to locate it, and be rewarded."
- Invite a volunteer to retrieve the box and remove the card.
- Select a volunteer to read aloud Jeremiah 29:13.
- Ask: "Does this verse sound familiar? We learned this verse in our Bible study time."
- Guide the group to say the verse together.
- Guide the children to close their eyes.
- Ask: "Can you see me with your eyes closed? Am I still in the room? Open your eyes."
- Explain: "When you close your eyes, you cannot see anything. Just because you closed your eyes and could not see me, does not mean I was not in the room. The same is true with God, just because we cannot see Him, does not mean He is not here. God is not hiding somewhere, waiting for us to find Him. He is everywhere. God said He will always be with us. He wants us to know where He is so we can experience Him."
- State: "Jeremiah 29:13 tells us when we seek (look for) God, we will find Him. God wants us to experience Him. Over the next eight weeks, we will learn more about experiencing God. As we learn about experiencing Him, we will learn how important it is to communicate with God. What do we call communicating with God? *(prayer)* We can pray about anything, anywhere, and at any time. We can also know God will hear and answer our prayers."
- Invite the children to share prayer requests.
- Pray for each child by name. Ask God to help each individual experience Him.

SUPPLIES AND PREP

Small decorative box; index card; marker; small, individually wrapped candy or small toys; bowl

- Write the words of Jeremiah 29:13 on the index card and place in the box.
- Hide the box out of sight.
- Place the prizes in the bowl.

ENGAGE OPTION THREE: WHAT DID GOD DO?

- Form three groups.
- Say: "I will assign your group a story to read and act out. As your group acts out the story, the rest of us will listen and discover what God did to help the situation."
- Assign each group a "What Did God Do?" story (pages 8–11).

SUPPLIES AND PREP

Index cards; Session 1 *Experiencing God Kids Learner Guide*

LEADER GUIDE **SESSION 1**

- Use index cards to bookmark John 14:26; 2 Timothy 3:16; Philippians 2:13; and 2 Corinthians 3:18b.

- Allow time for the groups to read and decide how to act out the stories.
- Invite the first group to read and act out its story.
- Ask: "What did God do to help the situation?"
- Read aloud the Bible verse listed at the bottom of the story page.
- Say: "We can trust God to help us in every situation."
- Continue for additional stories.
- Select a volunteer to read aloud John 14:26.
- Ask: "Who in the stories experienced God in this way?"
- Talk about how God helped the people know what to say and do.
- Read aloud 2 Timothy 3:16.
- Ask: "How does the Bible help us know what to do when we face difficult situations?"
- Select volunteers to read aloud Philippians 2:13 and 2 Corinthians 3:18b.
- Ask: "How do these verses apply to the stories?"
- Explain: "Sometimes God uses other people to speak to us and help us grow. We should listen to the people God places in our lives. These people can help us know about God and how we can experience Him."
- Say: "As we learn about experiencing God, we will learn how important it is to communicate with God. What do we call communicating with God? *(prayer)* We can pray about anything, anywhere, and at any time. We can also know God will hear and answer our prayers."
- Invite the children to share prayer requests.
- Pray for each child by name. Ask God to help each individual experience Him.

Ending The Lesson

- Say: "Today we began an amazing adventure. Hopefully this adventure will continue throughout the rest of our lives. During the next eight weeks we will discover how we can experience God. God wants to do amazing things in our lives. We can all know God and be a part of the adventure of working with Him."
- Call attention to "Experiencing God at Home" in the *Experiencing God Kids Learner Guide* (page 12).
- Explain: "This week, finish and review all the information in your booklet. Read the information printed on page 12 with your parents. Talk with them about the situations in 'What Did God Do?' "
- Invite the children to silently pray after you: "Dear God / Thank You for loving me. / Thank You that You want to have a relationship with me. / Help me to trust You. / Help me to listen to You. / Help me to see what You are doing around me. / Help me to experience You every day of my life. / Amen."
- Close in prayer, asking God to help each child experience Him this week.

PRAYER	SOLUTION
You had a problem and asked God to help you know what to do.	God gave you an idea or thought (wisdom) that helped you solve or get through the problem.
You asked God to let you be a part of His work.	You were asked to help in a new ministry at church where you were challenged to tell someone about Jesus.
You were upset and asked God to help you calm down.	As you thought about God, His peace made you feel better and helped you trust Him more.
For several months you prayed about something specific. You trusted God would take care of the situation for you. You began to feel God was not listening to you.	Just about the time you were ready to give up praying, something happened and you knew God answered your prayer.
You asked God to help you love your family and friends better.	During a difficult time with your family and friends, you felt God telling to you stop arguing, calm down, and listen. God helped you to love your family and friends.
You asked God to help you listen well at school, study hard, and do well.	You started enjoying school, studied more, and made better grades.
You asked God to help you be more respectful to your parents.	You noticed you are more obedient, helpful, and cooperative at home.
You asked God to help you get along with a kid who picks on you.	You got the courage to talk with the kid and discovered he really wanted someone to be his friend.
You prayed one of your friends would ask Jesus to be his Savior and Lord.	Your friend asked you how he could ask Jesus to be his Savior and Lord.
Someone asked you why you believe in Jesus. You asked God to know what to say.	As you started to speak, you knew exactly what to say to the person about why you believe in Jesus.
A friend asked you what she should do in a specific situation. You silently asked God to tell you what to say.	You knew exactly what to tell your friend. The advice you shared is what God told you to say.
Someone asked for prayer but did not tell you about his prayer request.	You prayed for the person, saying something like, "God, You know what this person needs. Please meet her needs."

Session 2:
GOD IS AT WORK

Teacher Preparation

BIBLE PASSAGE
2 Kings 6:8-23

BIBLE TRUTH
God is always at work around me.

LIFE APPLICATION
I can ask God to show me where He is at work around me and how I can be involved in what He is doing.

KEY VERSE
Deuteronomy 31:8

PRAYER CHALLENGE
Before beginning your planning, pray God will prepare your heart and work through you to speak to the children. Pray God will prepare the children to hear and apply what they learn so they can experience all He has planned for them.

- Read 2 Kings 6:8-23. As you read the events, note how God was at work even when the people did not notice His actions.

NOTICE THE INDIVIDUAL'S ACTIONS
- Elisha, successor to Elijah, was a prophet to Israel. He lived in the city of Dothan (DOH thuhn), northeast of Samaria (suh MEHR ih uh). He walked with God and had God's spirit upon him.
- King Jehoram (jih HOH ruhm), son of King Ahab (AY hab), was the ruler of the northern tribes of Israel. Just as his parents had done, he did evil in God's sight (2 Kings 3:2) including allowing the worship of Baal.
- King of Aram (AHR uhm) (Syria) waged war against Israel. Frustrated that the Israelites were receiving information about his plans through Elisha, he sent an army to Dothan to capture him.
- Elisha's servant, a young boy (Hebrew word *na'ar* translates young boy), even when faced with fear, witnessed firsthand the power of God at work.

NOTICE HOW GOD WAS AT WORK
- He protected His people.
- He revealed the Syrians' plans, allowing Elisha to send word to King Jehoram.
- He allowed the servant to see how He worked in the situation.
  Reread the events of 2 Kings 6:8-23. What decisions would you have made? Man's ways may be to take revenge and harm those who have done you wrong, but God's way is mercy and peace.
- Read 1 John 4:4. We can trust God because He is with us. He outnumbers any foes or problems we face. We learn to recognize what God is doing as we ask him to show us and became alert to His actions around us.
- Read Matthew 16:16-17; John 6:44; and John 16:8. What do these verses reveal as indicators that God is at work? These verses reveal God is at work when we see things that only He can do, the Holy Spirit reveals the truth of who Jesus is, and convicts individuals of sin. In addition, we know God is at work when He draws people to Himself. When people inquire about spiritual matters, wrestle with guilt because of their sins, or realizations of truths about God—God is at work.
- Place yourself in a child's situation. How does a child see God at work?

- Think about your life. As you read and study the Bible and daily walk with God, you learn to know and recognize how God does and does not work. You discover His true character and ways.

Getting Ready

- Welcome each child by name.
- Distribute *Experiencing God Kids Learner Guide* and pencils
- Guide the children to complete "Crack the Code" (page 1).
- Say: "Today we will discover God is always at work around us, even if we do not recognize His actions."
- Call attention to "Sammy and the Frogs" (page 3).
- Overview *Sammy Experiences God*.

Excite (5-8 MINUTES)

- Guide the children to stand in a circle.
- Select a volunteer to stand in the center.
- Explain: "I will hand a coin to someone. Without allowing the person in the middle of the circle to see, give the coin to the person next to you. Continue passing the coin to the right or left. When I say 'stop' the person in the middle will guess who has the coin. If he is correct, he changes places with the person holding the coin. After three incorrect guesses, we will reveal the coin and I will select another person to be in the center."
- Give the coin to a player.
- Play several rounds.
- Ask: "What made it difficult to know who had the coin?"
- Explain: "Even though we did not always see someone moving the coin, the coin changed hands. Sometimes things happen even when we do not see them. Today we will discover that God is always at work around us. Sometimes we see what God is doing, but there are times we do not recognize His actions. Why do we not notice some of the things God does?"
- Invite the children to respond.
- Display "Reality 1" poster.
- Select a volunteer to read aloud the poster.

Examine (10 MINUTES)

- Choose a volunteer to read aloud John 5:17.
- Ask: "What does this verse tell us about God?"
- State: "God is always at work around us, even when we do not recognize His actions."

SUPPLIES AND PREP

Bibles, Session 2 of *Experiencing God Kids Learner Guide* (1 per child), markers, crayons, tape, construction paper, pencils, coin, copy of *Sammy Experiences God* (ISBN 1433679809), "Reality 1" poster (Insert)

- Write the words of Deuteronomy 31:8 on the construction paper.

Sammy Experiences God is a classically illustrated children's book inspired by the *Experiencing God* teachings of Henry Blackaby.

CRACK THE CODE

I can ask God to show me where He is at work around me and how I can be involved in what He is doing.

TIP

Assist children with locating Bible passages.

LEADER GUIDE **SESSION 2**

- Guide the children to complete "Where Is God at Work?" (page 2).
- Invite the children to identify some of the places and actions they circled.
- Lead the children to open their Bibles to Deuteronomy 31:8.
- Select a volunteer to read aloud the verse.
- Encourage the children to complete "The Truth Is …" (page 3).
- Ask: "Which statements did you circle? Did you circle all of them? You should have, because all the statements are true."
- Display the verse poster.
- Continue: "Keep the words of this verse in mind as we listen to our Bible story."

Explore (25 MINUTES)

TIPS
- Write the individuals' names on a large sheet of paper.
- Provide name tags and Bible times clothing for the children to wear.

- Guide the children to open their Bibles to 2 Kings 6.
- Say: "The main individuals in our Bible story are the king of Aram, Elisha (the prophet), the king of Israel, and Elisha's servant (a young boy). Listen how God worked. After I tell the Bible story, we will act it out."
- Tell the Bible story in your own words.

GOD IS ALWAYS AT WORK

The king of Aram was at war with the nation of Israel. After talking with his officers, the king decided on a place to set up his camp.

Elisha sent word to the king of Israel, "The king of Aram is setting up his camp in this location." Elisha warned the king to beware of not only this location, but other places along the way the king had placed his camp.

This made the king of Aram extremely angry. He gathered his officers together and demanded to know who was the spy in his army. The king believed someone was telling the king of Israel about his plans.

One of the officers said, "None of us are telling the king of Israel your plans. The prophet Elisha, who lives in Israel, is telling the king everything you say."

The king of Aram ordered, "Go, find Elisha. I will send my army to capture him."

Someone reported to the king of Aram, "Elisha is in the city of Dothan."

The king of Aram sent horses, chariots, and a strong army to Dothan. Traveling at night, the army surrounded the city.

Early the next morning, Elisha's young servant boy got up and went outside. He saw the city surrounded by the Aramean army. The servant asked Elisha, "What should we do?"

Elisha told his servant, "Don't be afraid. We have more people on our side than the king of Aram has on his."

Elisha prayed for his servant, saying, "God, open the eyes of my servant so he can see." God allowed the servant to see the hills full of horses and chariots. As the army approached, Elisha prayed, "God, cause these men to become blind." God did just as Elisha asked, causing the king's army to become blind. Elisha said to the army, "This is not the place you are looking for. Follow me and I will take you to the right place." Elisha led the army to the city of Samaria.

After Elisha led the army to Samaria, he prayed, "God, open these men's eyes so they can see." Once again, God did as Elisha asked. When the men regained their sight, they realized they were in Samaria.

Upon seeing the king of Aram's army, the king of Israel asked Elisha, "Should I kill them?" Elisha told the king, "Since you did not capture them yourself, do not kill them. Feed them and allow them to return home to the king of Aram."

The king of Israel prepared a feast for the army. When the men finished eating, the king of Israel sent the men home. As a result of the king of Israel's actions, the king of Aram stopped fighting with Israel.

- Assign roles and dramatize the Bible story.
- Read aloud the following questions, inviting the children to respond. "How did the king of Israel know about the king of Aram's plans? What did Elisha's servant see when he went outside the next morning? What did the servant not see? Why couldn't he see the horses and chariots at first? How do you think he felt after he saw God's protection? When the king of Israel saw his enemy's army right before him, what did he ask Elisha? What advice did Elisha give him? Why was Elisha's advice a better plan?"
- Ask: "What can we learn from this Bible story?"
- Continue: "In what ways was God at work? Why could Elisha see the horses and chariots but the servant could not?"
- Inquire: "What did these individuals learn about God's working: the king of Aram, Elisha, the servant, the Aramean army, and the king of Israel?"
- Talk about the individuals and what they learned about God's actions.
- Direct the children to complete "Ways They Experienced God Working" (page 4).
- Ask: "Is God always at work around us? Do we always see what He is doing around us? How can we be involved in what God is doing around us?"
- Say: "Sometimes we are like the servant and do not see what God is doing. We may wonder, is God helping us? We can trust God is always at work around us. We can all be a part of what He is doing."
- Complete "Being a Part of What God Is Doing" (page 5).

WAYS THEY EXPERIENCED GOD WORKING

Elisha—God answered His prayers.
King of Aram—God revealed his plans to Elisha. His army was captured. As a result of the king of Israel's kindness, the king of Aram stopped fighting with Israel.
Servant—God allowed him to see things he could not see at first.
King of Israel—God allowed him to capture the Aramean army. He was kind to the army. As a result the king of Aram stopped fighting with Israel.
Aramean Army—They were blinded, led to Samaria, captured, fed, and released.

BEING A PART OF WHAT GOD IS DOING

- Read the Bible
- Pray
- Be willing for God to use you
- Ask God to show you where He is working
- Live in ways that please and honor God

LEADER GUIDE **SESSION 2**

events are common everyday activities. If we are not careful, people and events can keep us from following God's plan for our lives. God's plan is the best plan and His ideas are the best for our lives. We need to learn how to recognize what God is saying to us and to see what He is doing around us so we can follow Him."

SUPPLIES AND PREP

Session 2 of *Experiencing God Kids Learner Guide* (1 per child), pencils, large sheet of paper, marker, tape

- Secure the paper to the wall.

TIPS

- Write the words in the blanks (pages 8-9) as the children state them.
- Follow the margin list (page 25).

ENGAGE OPTION THREE: A CAPTAIN'S REPORT

- Explain: "I need your help writing a story. I will call out a type of word and select someone to tell me a word that fits the category. For example, if I say *place*, you could say *school, club house, grocery store*, or any other location. If you cannot think of a word, you can ask someone to help you."
- Open an *Experiencing God Kids Learner Guide* to pages 8-9.
- Work through the "Captain's Report" and call out the word types (underlines).
- Enlist an older child to write the words on the paper.
- Read aloud the story inserting the words the children stated.
- Ask: "Does this story make sense?"
- Say: "Let me read the story using the correct words (in bold)."
- Say: "In today's Bible story, the king of Aram sent his army to capture Elisha. The Bible does not tell us what the army captain told the king when he got back, but it must have been a pretty amazing story! Maybe his story went something like this."
- Read aloud the story.

CAPTAIN'S REPORT

To: The King of Syria

About: The mission to capture Elisha

Result: We failed, but had a really great dinner!

Report: Dear King,

As you know, you sent us to **Dothan** to capture **Elisha** because God was telling him where you were placing our **armies**. (I'm still a little unclear why you thought this plan would work. Obviously, God would tell Elisha [as usual] where we were.)

Anyway, we surrounded **Dothan** with **horses** and **chariots** and made it impossible for anyone in **Dothan** to **travel** anywhere. When the sun came up, we **mounted** our **horses** and were ready. I saw **Elisha's** servant. When the servant saw us, he **ran** into the **house**. When we saw **Elisha**, we got ready to **fight**. Then we saw **Elisha talking** to his **servant** and pointing to the **sky**. When we looked where he was pointing, we only saw **clouds**. We saw **Elisha** lift his **hands** and **pray**. That's when things changed. Suddenly, none of us knew where we were. None of us could **see**.

Getting Ready

- Place your hand on each child's shoulder as she enters the room and say, "I am so glad to see you. You are a special person. I love you, but more importantly, God loves you."
- Distribute *Experiencing God Kids Learner Guide* and pencils.
- Guide the children to complete "Crack the Code" (page 1).
- Ask: "How did it make you feel when I placed my hand on your shoulder and told you that I love you? How did it make you feel for me to say 'God loves you'?"
- Continue: "Today we will discover how much God loves us and wants a relationship with us."

Excite (5-8 MINUTES)

- Distribute bags and craft supplies.
- Instruct: "Write your name on the side of your bag."
- Guide each child to decorate his bag.
- Ask: "Have you ever heard the word *blessing*? What do you think about when you hear the word?"
- Invite the children to respond.
- Say: "When we hear the word *blessing* we may think of a prayer. We say a blessing before we eat, but the word *blessing* has another meaning. The second meaning is 'to honor God or a person with good words, or to praise someone.' A practice in the Bible was for fathers to bless their children, especially right before the fathers died."
- Distribute index cards.
- Continue: "Hearing someone say something nice about us means a lot. I want you to think about something you can say about the people in the room, but don't say anything out loud. Write your comments on the cards."
- Assist in writing notes.
- Say: "Place your cards in the bags for the persons you wrote about. We will read the comments later."
- Place the bags aside.

Examine (10 MINUTES)

- Explain: "Everyone stand up. I will call out a statement. If the statement applies to you, remain standing. If the statement does not apply to you, sit down. Let's see who is the last person standing."
- Call out statements such as, "I love people with brown hair," "I love people who are left-handed," "I love people who are eight years old."
- Continue calling out statements until only one person remains standing.
- Play several times.

LEADER GUIDE SESSION 3

SUPPLIES AND PREP

Bibles; Session 3 of *Experiencing God Kids Learner Guide* (1 per child); markers; crayons; tape; construction paper; pencils; lunch bags (1 per child); stickers, scissors, glue stick, other craft supplies to decorate bags; index cards (several per child); "Reality 2" poster (Insert)

- Write the words of John 3:16 on the construction paper, drawing blanks instead of the words *the world*.
- Write *God loves me* on individual index cards (1 per child).

TIPS

- Prepare a sample list of blessings.
- Prepare additional blessing cards to place in the children's bags (ensure each child has several cards).

CRACK THE CODE
I can know God loves me and wants a relationship with me.

TIP
Assist children in locating John 3:16 in their Bibles.

- Ask: "How did you feel when you had to sit down? Do you think I only love people with brown hair? How would you feel if that statement was true and you do not have brown hair? Would you feel unloved?"
- Select a volunteer to read aloud the "Crack the Code" message.
- Inquire: "How do you know God loves you? What would you say if someone said 'God only loves adults'?"
- Invite the children to respond.
- Guide the children to locate John 3:16 in their Bibles.
- Select a volunteer to read aloud the verse.
- Ask: "According to this verse, who does God love? Who is *the world*?"
- Guide the children to complete "The Bible Says …" (page 2).
- Comment: "The world includes all people, including everyone of us."
- Display the verse poster.
- Explain: "I will read aloud the verse, pausing at the blanks. When I pause, stand and shout out your name as loud as possible."
- Read aloud the verse, pausing at the blanks.
- Inquire: "What did God do because He loves us so much?"
- Continue: "God sent Jesus to earth so we could know Him and be forgiven of our sins. God wants each of us to ask Jesus to be our Savior and Lord. We will talk about this more later."
- Say: "I have a blessing for you to add to your bag. I will place a card in each person's hands. Do not look at the words until I instruct you to."
- Distribute prepared "God loves me" cards.
- Instruct: "On the count of three, everyone read aloud the words."
- Count to three and allow the children to read the words together.
- Say: "Do you believe these words? Let me hear you say the words like you believe them."
- Count to three and allow the children to read the words together.
- Repeat several times asking: "Girls, who does God love? *[Allow the girls to shout.]* Boys, who does God love? *[Allow the boys to shout.]* Everyone, who does God love?" *[Allow everyone to shout.]*
- Guide the children to place the cards in their bags.

Explore (25 MINUTES)

- Guide each child to select a partner.
- Say: "If you could be friends with any famous person, who would you like to know and why? Tell your partner."
- Ask: "Does this person know anything about you? Does he love you? Why or why not?"
- Continue: "Imagine I wanted to visit the leader of a country. Would I be able to walk up to his home and visit him? Who might stop me? What could happen to me?"
- Discuss the consequences of trying to approach a world leader's home.

- Explain: "I need your help during our Bible study. When you hear someone wanting to get close to Jesus, wave your hands in front of you and shout 'Go!' When you hear someone trying to stop the person, put your hands out in front of you and yell, 'Stop!' Let's practice."
- Practice the actions.
- Open your Bible to Mark 10:13-16.
- Tell the Bible story in your own words, pausing as indicated.

JESUS, THE DISCIPLES, AND THE CHILDREN

Jesus traveled with His disciples to towns and villages teaching people about God. The men arrived in an area called Judea. A large crowd of people came to listen to Jesus or to be healed. *[Pause.]*

Some people began to bring little children to Jesus. *[Pause.]* The people wanted Jesus to touch the children. *[Pause.]* The people's actions did not make the disciples happy. *[Pause.]* The disciples rebuked the people, trying to stop them from bringing the children to Jesus. *[Pause.]* When Jesus saw what the disciples were doing, He became upset. Listen to the what Jesus said to the disciples.

TIP
Define *rebuked* as "criticized sharply."

[Read aloud Mark 10:14-15. Pause.]

- Continue: "After saying these words, Jesus took the children in His arms, placed His hands on the children, and blessed them." *[Pause.]*
- Guide the children to complete "The Order Is …" (page 3).
- Review the Bible story and order of the pictures.
- Ask: "Why did the disciples want to stop the children from going to Jesus? How did Jesus respond to the disciples' actions? What did Jesus want the children to know? How did the children experience God?"
- Display "Reality 2" poster.
- Invite a volunteer to read aloud the poster.
- Ask: "How does it make you feel to know God loves you and wants to have a relationship with you?"
- Say: "God has given us so many things. He created a beautiful world for us to enjoy, gave us families and friends to care for us, created all types of animals to see, and gives us the things we need."
- Ask: "Do you remember the last part of John 3:16? What does this verse say we receive from God?" *(eternal life)*
- Direct the children to complete "God Loves Me This Much" (pages 4-5).
- Read aloud and talk about the ABCs of becoming a Christian.
- Say: "God's plan is for everyone to ask Jesus to be his Savior and Lord. To truly experience God, we must have a relationship with Him. The only way we can have a relationship with God is through Jesus' death, burial, and resurrection.

TIPS
- Be prepared to talk with each child individually about becoming a Christian.
- Plan to follow up with any child who asks Jesus to be His Savior and Lord.

LEADER GUIDE **SESSION 3**

God wants us to admit what we have done wrong (sin), believe Jesus is God's Son—that He died on the cross to provide a way for us to be forgiven of our sins, and confess our faith (belief) in Him as Savior and Lord. Some of us have made the decision to ask Jesus to be our Savior and Lord. If you have not, and would like to talk with me, I will be glad to talk with you."

- Pray, thanking God for the love He has for each person.
- Say: "Asking Jesus to be our Savior and Lord, is just the beginning of our relationship with God. We need to grow in our relationship."
- Direct the children to complete "Growing In My Relationship with God" (page 8).
- Talk about the various ways a person's relationship grows with God.
- Share a brief testimony of how your relationship with God grows and how it makes you feel to know God always loves you.

Engage (20 MINUTES)

SUPPLIES AND PREP
6 colors of construction paper, tape, marker
- Write *Start* on 1 sheet of paper. Write *The Spot* on another piece.
- Tape the construction paper on the floor in random order.

TIP
Make the game more challenging by using only 2 or 3 colors of paper.

ENGAGE OPTION ONE: TO THE SPOT
- Guide the children to line up behind the *Start* space.
- Say: "The object of the game is to make it to 'The Spot' or the end of the path. I will select one person to be the 'caller.' She will close her eyes while the other players step on the paper, one sheet at a time. You can move to any of the papers, but you must touch each paper in the path. When I say 'freeze,' stand still on a piece of paper. Without looking, the 'caller' will shout out a color. If you are standing on that color, you are safe, but everyone else must go back to 'Start' and begin again."
- Select a "caller."
- Guide her to stand to the side of the playing area with her back to the group and her eyes closed.
- Invite the children to step on each piece of paper as they move on the path.
- Allow the children to move for about five seconds, then state "freeze."
- Invite the "caller" to call out a color.
- Continue playing until one or more of the children reach "The Spot."
- Replay as time permits.
- Ask: "How did you feel when you had to go back to the beginning? How did the 'caller' affect the outcome of the game?"
- Ask: "Who tried to keep the children from reaching Jesus? Why? What happened when Jesus confronted the disciples? How do you think the children felt when the disciples tried to keep them away from Jesus?"
- Conclude: "We played a game to see who could reach 'The Spot' first. Having a relationship with God is not a game. We can know God loves us—everyone of us—and wants a relationship with us. When we begin that relationship, no one or no thing can keep us from God."
- Pray, thanking God for His love and the opportunity to have a relationship with Him.

ENGAGE OPTION TWO: TASTES OF THE WORLD
- Display the world map.
- Ask: "Have any of you ever traveled to or studied about another country? Show me where on the map you have traveled or studied."
- Allow the children to indicate places.
- Say: "Let's enjoy some foods from around the world."
- Guide the children to wash their hands.
- Serve the foods.
- Continue: "Let's test our knowledge about some eating habits around the world."
- Distribute pencils.
- Guide the children to answer the "Our World" questions (page 7).
- Ask: "Did you mark each statement true? You should have—they are all true!"
- Call attention to the recipes (page 6).
- Say: "Ask your parents to help you prepare these recipes for your family. As you eat the foods, pray for people all over the world who enjoy these types of food. Ask God to help the people know how much He loves them."
- Ask: "What type of foods do you think Jesus and the disciples ate?"
- Discuss Bible times foods.
- Review the Bible story.
- Call attention to the "Reality 2" poster.
- Comment: "God loves every one of us. He wants to have a relationship with us. What does it mean to have a relationship with someone?"
- Continue: "To have a relationship with someone means you get to know the person. You know what he likes and does not like. You know his strengths and weaknesses. You are able to share things with this person you may not share with someone else. Can you do these things with God? Do you know what God knows about you? He knows EVERYTHING!"
- Pray, thanking God for His love and the opportunity to have a relationship with Him.

SUPPLIES AND PREP
Various ethnic foods from around the world, plates, napkins, water, cups, world map, pencils, "Reality 2" poster, tape
- Prepare and post an allergy chart of foods.

TIPS
- Do not force children to taste the foods.
- Provide Bible times foods to taste and explore.

ENGAGE OPTION THREE: BE THE ARTIST
- Say: "Imagine a writer asked you to illustrate a book he wrote. The name of the book is *The Lonely King*."
- Distribute copies of *The Lonely King*.
- State: "Let's take turns reading aloud the book."
- Guide the children to take turns reading aloud.
- Review the details of the story.
- Ask: "Can you tell me the meaning of the story?"
- Explain: "God is like the king. God wants a relationship with us. He does not want us to repeat the same prayers over and over again. He wants us to talk with Him and tell Him how we feel, what we think, what we are struggling with, as well as what makes us happy."
- State: "Johnny did not just show the king respect, he showed him love as well. When Johnny was honest with the king and told him how much he loved him, the king heard and honored him."

SUPPLIES AND PREP
Markers, colored pencils, crayons, stapler/staples, "Reality 2" poster
- Copy, fold, and staple copies of "The Lonely King" (pages 92-95) (1 per child).

TIPS
- Be sensitive to the children's reading levels.
- Do not force a child to read aloud.

LEADER GUIDE **SESSION 3**

- Review the Bible story.
- Call attention to the "Reality 2" poster.
- Comment: "God loves every one of us. He wants to have a relationship with us. What does it mean to have a relationship with someone?"
- Continue: "To have a relationship with someone means you get to know the person. You know what he likes and does not like. You know his strengths and weaknesses. You are able to share things with this person you may not share with someone else. Can you do these things with God? Do you know what God knows about you? He knows EVERYTHING!"
- Pray, thanking God for the opportunity to have a relationship with Him.
- Distribute colored pencils, markers, and crayons.
- Guide the children to illustrate their books.
- Suggest the children read their books to their families this week.

Ending The Lesson

SUPPLIES AND PREP
Scissors
- Copy "Blessing Strips" (Insert) (1 page per child).

- Say: "In our Bible study time, we wrote notes of blessing. Let's give some more blessing statements to our friends."
- Distribute "Blessing Strips" and scissors.
- Guide the children to cut apart the strips.
- Say: "Read each statement. Think about whom the statement best describes. Place the statement in the person's bag."
- Assist as needed.
- Encourage the children to silently read the statements in their bags.
- Ask: "How does it make you feel that your friends said these things about you?"
- Allow the children to respond.
- Continue: "If God wrote something on a piece of paper and placed it in your bag, what would He say? I know one thing God would say to everyone of us, 'I love you.'"
- Call attention to the "Reality 2" poster.
- Ask: "How do we know God loves us?"
- Say: "God wants to bless us and show us His love every day. He also wants us to show Him our love by obeying Him, spending time with Him, and showing love to other people. God knows it is not always easy to love everyone, but He expects us to do our best. We should love our families, friends, teachers, neighbors, and so forth. What are some ways we can love people?"
- Discuss various ways to love people.
- Call attention to "Love Them Too" (page 9).
- Challenge the children to complete each of the actions this week.
- Call attention to "Experiencing God at Home" in the *Experiencing God Kids Learner Guide* (page 12).
- Explain: "This week, finish and review all the information in your booklet. Talk with your parents about what you experience."
- Pray, thanking God for His love.

> HOW DOES IT MAKE YOU FEEL TO KNOW GOD LOVES YOU AND WANTS A RELATIONSHIP WITH YOU?

Session 4:
GOD WANTS ME TO BE A PART OF HIS WORK

Teacher Preparation

BIBLE PASSAGE
John 6:1-15

BIBLE TRUTH
God wants me to be a part of His work.

LIFE APPLICATION
I can learn to recognize when God is inviting me to be a part of what He is doing.

KEY VERSE
Ephesians 2:10

PRAYER CHALLENGE
Before beginning your planning, pray God will prepare your heart and work through you to speak to the children. Pray God will prepare the children to hear and apply what they learn so they can experience all He has planned for them.

- Read Matthew 14:13-21, Mark 6:30-51, Luke 9:10-17, and John 6:1-15. Compare and contrast the same event recorded in all four gospels.
- Notice details included in Matthew 14:1-12, Mark 6:14-29, and Luke 9:7-9. Jesus learned of the beheading of John the Baptist. Jesus withdrew for some personal time with God. However, many people wanted Jesus' attention. The people even followed Him across the Sea of Galilee.
- Reread John 6:5-6. Notice Jesus had compassion for the people. The disciples had suggested sending them away to find food. Notice Jesus' response. He instructed the disciples to feed the people. His directions confused the disciples, how could they feed so many people? Though the disciples saw the situation through human eyes, God had a different plan. Jesus' actions taught the disciples to surrender what they had and trust God to supply the rest.
- Reflect on the details in the story. Andrew found the boy (meaning under the age of 13) with five barley loaves and two fish. Barley was considered an inferior type of bread. By having barley loaves, the boy was most likely from a poor family. The fish were most likely dried or pickled. Nothing is mentioned of the boy's family. Was he there alone? A boy his age would normally have been in the synagogue school or working at home in the family trade or on the farm. Why had the boy followed Jesus? Perhaps he was intrigued by Jesus' teachings and miracles. Whatever the reason, the boy was willing to give all his lunch to Jesus. The request for food was God's invitation to the boy to be a part of what God was doing.
- Imagine the reaction of the disciples and the young boy as Jesus prayed and then took the bread and began to feed the people. The food multiplied until everyone had eaten as much as desired. Twelve baskets of leftovers remained. What seemed an insignificant offering in the face of such a great need became the means for God to demonstrate His power.
- Reread John 6:14-15. How did the people respond to Jesus? The people were so amazed they wanted to make Jesus their king. Jesus knew His purpose was not to be an earthly king, but to fulfill the will of His Father.
- Think about your life. What have you given to God to use? In what ways has He multiplied your offerings to impact the lives of people around you? What did God teach you through your faith? What "leftovers" has God provided for you?
- Thank God for the invitation He has given you to be a part of what He is doing in the lives of the children. Ask God to use you for whatever and however He needs.

EXPERIENCING GOD AT HOME **KIDS**

Getting Ready

- Greet each child.
- Distribute *Experiencing God Kids Learner Guide* and pencils.
- Guide the children to complete "Crack the Code" (page 1).
- Ask: "If you could be famous for something, what would you want it to be?"
- Allow the children to discuss what they would like to be famous for doing.
- Say: "We may never be famous movie stars or singers, but we can be a part of something more important. We can be a part of what God is doing."
- Continue: "Today we will discover how a willingness to give up his lunch was all a young boy needed to be a part of what God was doing."

Excite (5-8 MINUTES)

- Ask: "Have you ever received an invitation to a birthday party or another event? How did it make you feel being invited to go somewhere?"
- Invite the children to respond.
- Continue: "Imagine you get to invite someone to a special event. Look at 'You're Invited' (page 2) in your booklets. Fill in the missing information on the invitation."
- Assist as needed.
- Guide the children to state some of the places they invited their friends.
- Say: "Let's act out some activities we can be invited to. I will choose a child to pick an invitation card. The card will tell him what is he inviting everyone to attend. He cannot use any words, only actions."
- Select a child.
- Guide her to pick a card and act out the event.
- Continue for additional cards as time permits.
- Ask: "How would you respond if you received an invitation saying, 'God invites you to be a part of what He is doing'? Would you look forward to being a part of God's actions? Why or why not?"

Explore (25 MINUTES)

- Select a volunteer to read aloud the "Crack the Code" message.
- Ask: "What age does a person have to be before God can use him?"
- Invite the children to respond.
- Continue: "Today we're going to learn about a boy God used in one of Jesus' miracles. As you listen to the Bible story, pretend to be a detective searching for clues. Your task is to discover the problem, the disciples' solution, and God's solution."
- Call attention to the paper.

SUPPLIES AND PREP

Bibles, Session 4 *Experiencing God Kids Learner Guide* (1 per child), pencils, "Reality 3" poster (Insert), colored pencils, marker, masking tape, index cards, various colors of construction paper, scissors, clothespins (2 per word of Ephesians 2:10), 2 long strings, 4 chairs, large sheet of paper, goldfish crackers, bread, water, cups, napkins

- Write *You are invited to a* _____ (wedding, birthday party, baseball game, sleepover, baby shower, etc.) (1 statement per card).
- Write the words of Ephesians 2:10 on a sheet of construction paper.
- Cut 2 sets of fish shapes (page 88) (1 color per set), 1 for each word of Ephesians 2:10. Write 1 word per fish.
- Tie the strings between chairs, creating fishing lines to attach the fish.
- Secure the paper to the wall. Write *Problem, Disciples' Solution,* and *God's Solution* on the paper.

CRACK THE CODE

I can learn to recognize when God is inviting me to be a part of what He is doing.

- Open your Bible to John 6:1-15.
- Tell the Bible story in your own words.

A BOY'S LUNCH

TIP

Bold phrases are answers to "My Findings" (page 3).

For some time, Jesus had been teaching as well as healing people. This caused many people to follow Him. Even when Jesus crossed to the other side of the Sea of Galilee, the people continued to follow Him. Jesus and the disciples went up **on a mountain** and sat down. When Jesus looked up, He saw a large crowd of people coming toward Him.

Jesus asked Philip, **"Where can we buy bread to feed these people?"** Jesus already knew what He was going to do, but **He asked Philip this to test him**.

- Ask: "What was the problem?"
- Record the response on the paper.

Philip answered, **"Several month's of pay would not buy enough bread for all of these people to even have a small bite."**

Andrew, Simon Peter's brother, spoke up saying, **"There is a boy here with his lunch of five barley loaves and two small fish,** but that is not enough food for all of these people."

- Ask: "What was the disciples' solution?"
- Record the response on the paper.

Jesus told the disciples to have the people sit down. **About 5,000 men** were in the crowd (not counting the women and children). **Jesus took the bread, gave thanks to God, and began giving everyone pieces of it. Jesus gave the people as much bread as they wanted. Then He did the same thing with the fish.**

After the people finished eating, Jesus instructed the disciples, **"Collect the leftovers, don't let anything be wasted."** The disciples collected **12 baskets of leftovers**.

- Ask: "What was the disciples' solution?"
- Record the response on the paper.
- State: "When the people saw what Jesus had done, they said to themselves, 'This Man is the Prophet we have been looking for.' Jesus knew the people wanted to make Him their king, so He left and went to a mountain by Himself."
- Ask: "What did you discover from the Bible story?"
- Review the problem and solutions.

- Discuss: "If you were one of the disciples, do you think you would have had the same solution? Would you have thought one little boy's lunch could feed all the people?"
- Serve the goldfish crackers and bread.
- Read aloud "My Findings" (page 3) questions, inviting the children to respond.
- Ask: "How does it make you feel to know God used a young boy's lunch to feed all of the people? What part did the boy play in this miracle?"
- Continue: "The boy was willing for Jesus to use his lunch to feed the people. What do you think the boy thought as Jesus prayed, broke the bread, and fed all of the people? How would you have responded?"
- Say: "God still uses children to do great things. Let's read about how God used a girl named Juliana to do something amazing."
- Invite volunteers to read aloud "Juliana's Story" (pages 4-5).
- Ask: "What was God's invitation to Juliana's family? How did they respond? How have other people in Canada responded to God's invitation to be a part of what He is doing on Nativity Hill?"
- Discuss how God used Juiliana, her family, and other people to minister at Nativity Hill.
- Guide the children to locate Ephesians 2:10 in their Bibles.
- Select a volunteer to read aloud the verse.
- Define terms or concepts the children do not understand.
- Display the verse poster.
- Say: "Let's play a game to help us remember this verse."
- Form two teams.
- Place the fish (words facedown) at one end of the room.
- Direct the teams to stand at the opposite end of the room.
- Assign each team a color. Call attention to the "fishing lines."
- Say: "Printed on these fish are the words to our Bible verse. One person from your team will run to the 'pond' and locate the fish with the first word of the verse on it. Return to your team and clothespin the fish to the 'fishing line.' The next person will then race to the 'pond' and locate the next word. Continue until you get all the fish in order on your 'fishing line.'"
- Run the race.
- Congratulate the children on their efforts.
- Guide the teams to read aloud the verse.
- Ask: "How does this verse relate to the events in our Bible story? What had God caused to happen in advance of Jesus feeding the people?"
- Ask: "What did God cause to happen in Juliana's story?"
- Say: "God has a plan for each of our lives. He wants us to be a part of the things He is doing. God asks, or invites, each of us to join Him."
- Display "Reality 3" poster.
- Select a volunteer to read aloud the poster.
- Inquire: "What are some things God may be inviting us to do?"
- Invite the children to complete "What I Can Do" (page 6).
- Discuss ways children can be involved in what God is doing.

TIP
Ensure the words on the fish remain facedown.

- Ask: "How can we respond to God's invitation?"
- Guide the children to form small groups, one group per adult leader.
- Explain: "Our prayer time is going to be different today. We are going to place our hands on each person individually and pray for him."
- Guide one child to stand in the center of the group.
- Direct each child to place one hand on the person in the center of the group.
- Select a volunteer to pray specifically for the child by name.
- Continue until each child is prayed for.
- Close the prayer time, thanking God for His invitation to be a part of His work.

Engage (20 MINUTES)

SUPPLIES AND PREP
Bibles, colored pencils, Session 4 *Experiencing God Kids Learner Guide* (1 per child)

ENGAGE OPTION ONE: GOD'S PLAN FOR ME POETRY
- Guide the children to open their Bibles to Psalm 139.
- Select a volunteer to read aloud verses 14-18.
- Say: "These words were written by King David. What do you remember about David?"
- Recall facts related to David. *(killed Goliath; played the harp for King Saul; refused to kill King Saul; was best friends with Saul's son, Jonathan; was the father of King Solomon)*
- Ask: "What do you think David thought as we wrote these words? What plans did God have for David? How did David respond to God's invitation?"
- Say: "King David wrote many of the psalms contained in the Book of Psalms. Many times he used poetry to express his ideas. Let's read a modern-day writing of Psalm 139:14-18."
- Invite a volunteer to read aloud the poem "Me" (page 7).
- Say: "Let's write poems about our relationship with God and how we can join Him in His work."
- Distribute colored pencils.

TIP
Share a brief testimony of how you are joining God in His work.

- Guide the children to write a poem based on God's plans for their lives (page 7).
- Assist as needed.
- Invite the children to read aloud their poems.
- Continue: "Was it possible for the young boy to feed over 5,000 people with his lunch? Does God ever ask us to do something that is impossible?"
- Explain: "Sometimes God may ask us to do something that we think is impossible. Let's read Luke 1:37."
- Select a volunteer to read aloud Luke 1:37.
- Ask: "What does this verse tell us about God?"
- Say: "God is inviting us to be a part of the things He is doing. He wants us to listen to and obey Him. This week, look for what God is doing in your neighborhood, school, family, church, or other places. Ask God to show you what you can do to be a part of His work, and then join Him."
- Pray for God's guidance and direction.

ENGAGE OPTION TWO: WHAT CAN I DO?

- Form three groups.
- Ask: "Have you ever had someone ask you for advice? You may have helped someone know what to do in a difficult situation. Let's see how well you can give advice. Imagine you are on television. One person in your group will present a situation. Your group must present a drama helping the person know how to respond."
- Distribute "Situation" strips.
- Assist the children in deciding how to deal with the situations.
- Invite each group to present the drama.
- Summarize the situations and group responses.
- Continue: "Does God ever ask us to do something impossible?"
- Explain: "Sometimes God may ask us to do something we think is impossible. Let's read Luke 1:37."
- Select a volunteer to read aloud Luke 1:37.
- Ask: "What does this verse tell us about God?"
- Say: "God is inviting us to be a part of the things He is doing. He wants us to listen to and obey Him. This week, look for what God is doing in your neighborhood, school, family, church, or other places. Ask God to show you what you can do to be a part of His work, and then join Him."
- Pray for God's guidance and direction.

SUPPLIES AND PREP
Scissors
- Copy and cut apart "Situations" (page 97).

TIP
Share a brief testimony of how you are joining God in His work.

ENGAGE OPTION THREE: WORK TOGETHER

- Ask: "Have you ever had a difficult task to complete? Did you wish you had someone to help you? Let's see how well we work together."
- Guide the children to form two teams.
- Display the box of items.
- Explain: "Without speaking loud enough for the other team to hear, decide how quickly you think your team can match all of the items in this box. Everyone on your team must help match the items."
- Allow the teams to discuss their times.
- Invite one team to state the amount of time needed.
- Ask the other team, "Do you think you can match all of the items faster? If so, how fast can you complete the task?"
- Explain: "We will continue reducing the time until one team feels it cannot match all of the items in the stated amount of time. The team will shout, 'Work Together!' The other team must work together to match the items. If your team is successful, you earn 1,000 points. If you are not successful, the other team earns the points."
- Play the first round.
- Add two or three additional items to the box and replay.
- Continue as time permits.

SUPPLIES AND PREP
Large box, 2 matching items (pair of socks, water bottles, keys, paper clips, rubber bands, rings, so forth), stopwatch
- Place about half of the matching items in the box. Add the remaining items as the game continues.

TIP
Share a brief testimony of how you are joining God in His work.

LEADER GUIDE **SESSION 4**

- Ask: "How did you decide how quickly you could match the items? When the other team stated their time, did you think it was impossible? Why?"
- Discuss the responses.
- Continue: "Was it possible for the young boy's lunch to feed over 5,000 people? Does God ever ask us to do something impossible?"
- Explain: "Sometimes God may ask us to do something we think is impossible. Let's read Luke 1:37."
- Select a volunteer to read aloud Luke 1:37.
- Ask: "What does this verse tell us about God?"
- Say: "God is inviting us to be a part of the things He is doing. He wants us to listen to and obey Him. This week, look for what God is doing in your neighborhood, school, family, church, or other places. Ask God to show you what you can do to be a part of His work, and then join Him."
- Pray for God's guidance and direction.

Ending The Lesson

- Say: "Around the room are bags with treats in them. You and your partner may select one of the bags and enjoy the treat inside. However, before you enjoy the treat, you both must complete the action attached to the bag. Which bag you and your partner select first is the action you must complete. After completing your action, come back to your seats and enjoy the snack together."
- Allow the children to select bags, complete the actions, and return to their seats to enjoy the snacks.
- Ask: "Was it easy to complete your task? Why or why not?"
- Select a volunteer to read aloud "Reality 3" poster.
- Choose a volunteer to read aloud the Ephesians 2:10 poster.
- Recall the actions of the young boy in the Bible story.
- Say: "The young boy did not have a lot—all he had was his lunch. Because he was willing to give his lunch to Jesus, over 5,000 people were fed. What do you have that God can use? Are you willing to give it to Him? What do you think God can do with the things you give Him?"
- Guide the children to silently reflect on the questions.
- Pray, asking God to help the children to be willing do what He asks, give what they have, and obey God in everything they do and say.
- Call attention to "Joining God's Team" (page 8).
- Say: "God will not force you to join Him in what He is doing. This week, read the information on this page. Seriously think about the commitment you can make to join God. If you are serious about joining God in what He is doing, sign and date the pledge."
- Call attention to "Experiencing God at Home" in the *Experiencing God Kids Learner Guide* (page 12).

SUPPLIES AND PREP
Paper lunch bags (1 per every 2 children), scissors, tape, goldfish crackers (or other snack)
- Print "Statements" (Insert). Cut apart and tape 1 statement to each bag.
- Place goldfish crackers in the bags. Tape the bags closed.

TIP
Guide the children to wash their hands before enjoying the snacks.

ARE YOU SERIOUS ABOUT JOINING GOD IN HIS WORK?

SESSION 4

LEADER GUIDE **SESSION 4**

Session 5:
GOD SPEAKS, I LISTEN

Teacher Preparation

BIBLE PASSAGE
1 Samuel 3:1-11,19

BIBLE TRUTH
God speaks and shows me what He wants me to do.

LIFE APPLICATION
I can hear God speaking to me personally and know He will show me what He wants me to do.

KEY VERSE
Jeremiah 29:11

PRAYER CHALLENGE
Before beginning your planning, pray God will prepare your heart and work through you to speak to the children. Pray God will prepare the children to hear and apply what they learn so they can experience all He has planned for them.

- Read 1 Samuel 3:1-11,19. Notice how God spoke to Samuel.
- Reflect on Hannah's prayer for a baby (1 Samuel 1:1-2:11). What did Hannah promise God if He would give her a son? How did Hannah fulfill her promise?
- Reread 1 Samuel 3:1. At this point in his life, Samuel was being raised by Eli, the priest at Shiloh (SHIGH loh), the location of the tabernacle. At this time in Israel's history, there was little direct word from God.
- Reread verse 7. Up to this time in his life, Samuel did not know God. God's Word had never been revealed to him. He learned to recognize God's voice as God spoke to him and as his relationship with God grew. Think about how you learned to recognize God's voice. We learn to recognize God speaking to us as we walk in relationship with Him and get to know Him better.
- Reread verse 10. God came and stood near Samuel. Regardless of whether Samuel saw a physical presence, a vision, or merely experienced a closer, more tangible presence of God, we do know his encounter with God was more than hearing a voice. God literally came near Samuel.
- Read 1 Samuel 3:11-18. Samuel responded as Eli had instructed him with a willingness to listen and obey. God revealed His plan to bring judgment on Eli and his sons for their disobediences. God was beginning to prepare Samuel to one day assume the role of prophet and priest in Israel.
- Read 1 Samuel 3:19–4:1. Samuel grew in his knowledge of God and continued to receive revelations from God.
- Think about your life. How does God speak to you? God can speak any way He chooses—prayer, Bible study, circumstances, other people, or events in your life. When circumstances in life line up, that can be God speaking to you. When you spend time in prayer, and specific Scriptures or persons to mind, that can be God speaking to you. When you receive wise counsel from godly people, that can be God speaking to you. When you hear something you believe is from God, ask Him to confirm what you are hearing. God will not speak contrary to His Word.
- Read John 10:27. Jesus stated that His sheep know His voice. Our ability to hear the voice of God is a result of our daily walk with Him. As we spend time with Him in Bible study and prayer, we come to know God's voice.

- Ask yourself, how well do I recognize God's voice? How obedient am I to respond to what He tells me? What needs to change in my life to more obediently follow His plans for me?

Getting Ready

- Greet each child by name.
- Distribute *Experiencing God Kids Learner Guide* and pencils.
- Guide the children to complete "Crack the Code" (page 1).
- Say: "I called you by name when you came into the room. How did it make you feel to hear your name? When your parents call you by your whole name, how do you feel?"
- Invite the children to respond.

SUPPLIES AND PREP

Bibles, Session 5 *Experiencing God Kids Learner Guide* (1 per child), pencils, "Reality 4" poster (Insert), blindfold, construction paper, marker, tape

- Write *Bible, People, Prayer, Circumstances* on construction paper (1 word per page).
- Write the words of Jeremiah 29:11 on a piece of construction paper.

Excite (5-8 MINUTES)

- Say: "Let's play a game to see how well we recognize people's voices. I will select someone to blindfold and stand at the opposite end of the room. I will then select someone to call out the person's name and say, 'Can you guess who I am?' If I pick you to speak, disguise your voice so it is more difficult for the blindfolded person to guess who is speaking."
- Select a child to stand at the end of the room and blindfold.
- Pick a child to say, "_____ (blindfolded child's name), can you guess who I am?"
- Allow the blindfolded child three guesses to figure out who called his name.
- Reveal who spoke.
- Select additional children to blindfold and children to speak.
- Continue as time permits.
- Ask: "Was it easy to know who was calling your name? Why or why not? How would you respond if you heard someone call your name, but the person is not in the room?"
- Say: "We knew who was calling our names because we know what each person's voice sounds like. How would you respond if God called your name?"

Examine (10 MINUTES)

- Say: "Today we will learn about the importance of listening. If we are not careful, we cannot hear what God wants to say to us. Let's test our hearing. I will read aloud a story, then I will ask you some questions."
- Read aloud "My Day at the Farm."

LEADER GUIDE **SESSION 5**

MY DAY AT THE FARM

O, what a beautiful morning. Three black birds flew across the bright blue sky. Six yellow ducks made their way across the clear lake. My grandmother, dressed in her red shirt, blue jeans, and brown shoes gathered eggs from the chicken coop. Every morning she would gather about 20 eggs. She used most of the eggs to cook breakfast for our family. My job was to help my grandfather harvest corn. The corn stalks were taller than me, so I picked the ears of corn I could reach. My grandfather picked the rest.

- Say: "Let's see how well you listened. I will call someone's name and ask her a question. After hearing the answer, stand up if you think she is correct. Stay seated if she is incorrect."
- Select individuals to answer the questions. Invite the children to stand or stay seated.
- Ask questions such as:
  → How many birds were flying across the sky? *(3)*
  → What color were the birds? *(black)*
  → How many ducks were on the lake? *(6)*
  → What color shirt was grandfather wearing? *(does not state)*
  → How many eggs did grandmother gather? *(about 20)*
  → What job did the narrator have? *(to help grandfather harvest corn)*
- Congratulate the children on their listening abilities.
- Say: "Sometimes it is easy to listen and remember things. At other times it is not. Open your Bible to 1 Samuel 3. Let's discover how God spoke to a small boy named Samuel."

Explore (25 MINUTES)

- Say: "Today we will learn about a boy who heard God speak to him. This boy's mother, Hannah, had prayed for a long time to have a baby. She promised God if He would answer her prayer, she would dedicate her baby to serve God. God answered her prayers. When Samuel was old enough, Hannah took him to live with the priest, Eli. One night, something amazing happened to Samuel."
- Continue: "I need someone to pretend to be Samuel and someone to be Eli."
- Select two volunteers.
- Assign roles.
- Guide "Samuel" to lay down on one side of the room and "Eli" on the opposite.
- Instruct the volunteers: "Listen as I tell the Bible story. When you hear what Samuel or Eli did, get up and act out the actions."
- Continue: "I need everyone to speak to 'Samuel.' When I point to you, whisper 'Samuel, Samuel.' Let's practice."
- Point to the children and encourage them to whisper, "Samuel, Samuel."
- Open your Bible to 1 Samuel 3.
- Tell the Bible story in your own words.

SAMUEL HEARD GOD SPEAK TO HIM

When Samuel was a small boy, his mother, Hannah, took him to live and serve with the priest, Eli. During this time, God rarely spoke to Eli or anyone else. One night, Eli, who has going blind, was lying down where he usually slept. The lamp had gone out, and Samuel was lying down in the tabernacle. God spoke to Samuel. *[Point to the children.]*

Samuel said, "Here I am." He got up, ran to Eli, and said, "I'm here. Did you need me?" *[Direct "Samuel" to run to "Eli."]*

Eli said, "I did not call you, go back to bed." *[Direct "Eli" to speak to "Samuel."]*

Samuel went back to bed. *[Direct "Samuel" to return to where he began.]*

Again, God called Samuel. *[Point to the children.]* Once again, Samuel got up and ran to Eli. *[Direct "Samuel" to run to "Eli."]*

Again, Eli told Samuel he did not call him and to go back to bed. *[Direct "Samuel" to return to where he began.]*

Up to this point in his life, Samuel had never heard God calling him, so he did not recognize God's voice.

A third time, God called Samuel *[point to the children]* and once again, he ran to Eli. *[Direct "Samuel" to run to "Eli."]*

Finally, Eli knew God was calling Samuel. Eli told Samuel, "Go back to bed. If God calls you again, say, 'Speak, Lord. I am listening.'" Samuel did just as Eli instructed. *[Direct "Samuel" to return to where he began.]*

God came and stood near Samuel, calling out "Samuel, Samuel." *[Point to the children.]*

Samuel said, "I am listening." *[Guide "Samuel" to listen.]*

God told Samuel what He was going to do to the nation of Israel.

- Say: "God was with Samuel as he grew. Samuel did not forget anything God told him."
- Thank the volunteers and allow them to return to their seats.
- Ask: "Who did Samuel think was calling him? Why did Samuel not know God was calling him? Who helped Samuel recognize God was speaking to him?"
- Guide the children to complete "What God Said to Samuel" (page 2).
- Ask: "What did God say to Samuel?"

WHAT GOD SAID TO SAMUEL
I am about to do something amazing in Israel.

LEADER GUIDE **SESSION 5**

CRACK THE CODE
I can learn to understand when God is speaking to me.

HOW GOD SPEAKS TO ME
Bible
Prayer
People
Circumstances

MATCH IT UP
Peter—Acts 10:9-16
Abram—Gen. 15:1-6
Moses—Exodus 33:8-11
Josiah—2 Kings 22:3-13
Paul—Acts 27:23-26
Jacob—Gen. 28:10-16
Daniel—Daniel 2:26-30
Deborah—Judges 4:4-8

- Display "Reality 4" poster.
- Invite a volunteer to read aloud the poster.
- Say: "You discovered a message when you came into the classroom today. What did you discover on the 'Crack the Code?'"
- Select a volunteer to read aloud the "Crack the Code" message.
- Ask: "Does God speak to people today? If so, in what ways?"
- Direct the children to complete "How God Speaks to Me" (page 3).
- Talk about ways God speaks to people.
- Say: "God has something personal to say to each of us. He wants to tell us what He wants us to do. We learn to listen to God when we spend time with Him and get to know Him better."
- Display the *Bible, People, Prayer,* and *Circumstances* signs randomly around the room.
- Say: "I will read aloud a situation. Decide how God spoke to the person and go stand under that sign."
- Read aloud a "How God Spoke" (page 99) situation.
- Guide the children to stand near the sign they feel describes how God spoke.
- Invite a few children to indicate why they selected the method.
- Continue for additional situations as time permits.
- Say: "Let's discover how God spoke to some people in the Bible."
- Guide the children to complete "Match It Up!" (page 4).
- Reveal the answers.
- Say: "If we read the rest of 1 and 2 Samuel, we would discover how God worked through Samuel. God had a plan for Samuel's life."
- Invite the children to complete "Follow the Steps and Know the Plan" (page 9).
- Select a volunteer to read aloud Jeremiah 29:11.
- Display the "Jeremiah 29:11" poster.
- Say: "Let's pretend we are the prophet Jeremiah saying these words."
- Guide the children to say the words as Jeremiah may have stated them.
- Direct the children to stand in a circle.
- Continue: "Let's make the verse more personal. Each person will say the verse, inserting the name of the person standing to your right. For example, I will say, 'I know the plans I have for Carrington,' and the rest of the verse. We will continue around the circle until each person's name is stated."
- Say the verse.
- Ask: "How does it make you feel to know God has a plan for your life? Are you willing to follow God's plan? Why or why not?"
- Conclude: "Silently pray for the person standing on your left. Ask God to help him listen to and obey everything God says."
- Pause as the children pray, then close the prayer time.

Engage (20 MINUTES)

ENGAGE OPTION ONE: DOES THAT SOUND LIKE GOD?
- Recall the name game played in "Excite."
- Say: "A study by Canadian and Chinese researchers found that even before being born, babies can recognize their mothers' voices. Learning to recognize when God is speaking to us is important. We do not want to miss what He says. Let's see how well we can recognize what God may say to someone. I will read aloud a situation. If you believe this is something God would do, cup your hands behind your ears. If it is not something God would say, place your hands over your mouth."
- Read aloud the statements, one at a time. Invite the children to indicate why they responded as they did.
    - → Paige was upset that her mom would not let her watch television. Paige was about to say something unkind to her mom when she remembered she should honor and obey her mother. Instead of saying anything, Paige silently prayed for a better attitude.
    - → Seth loves doughnuts! He believes God will give him a job in a doughnut place so he can eat dozens every day.
    - → Kiryn prayed for wisdom about what classes she should take in school. The more she thought about her classes, the more she knew the right choice. She talked to her parents and they agreed.
    - → Becca had a scary dream. She woke up wondering what the dream meant. She wondered if God was telling her something.
    - → Anderson was angry. A bully at school picked on him and his friends all day. Anderson thought about David and Goliath and imagined what it would take for Anderson to defeat the bully.
    - → Mark realized God did not want him to see the bully get hurt. Mark prayed for wisdom and for the bully. Mark told his parents what had happened and his dad suggested that Mark and his friend play on another playground. The next day, the bully did not bother Mark and his friends.
    - → Alice and her mother were watching the evening news. An upset woman on the news stated, "Some things can never be forgiven!" Alice knew the woman's comments did not match what the Bible taught.
    - → Gary really wanted to see the latest sci-fi movie all his friends were seeing. He asked God to help him see the movie. Gary saved money to buy a ticket, but when he told his parents what movie he wanted to see, they said no. One of Gary's friends invited him to a sleepover and to see the movie. Gary's parents would never know about him seeing the movie. Gary thought God was answering his prayer.
- Select a volunteer to read aloud Jeremiah 29:11.
- Ask: "How can these situations help us know about God's plans?"
- Say: "God does not want to punish us or keep us from having fun. God knows what is best for us. When we follow His plans, we experience things that people who do not follow God cannot. We can know what God says to us."
- Pray for each child to listen and respond to what God says to him and wants him to do.

SUPPLIES AND PREP
No supplies are needed for this activity.

TIP
Make the activity more active by allowing the children to act out the statements as TV talk shows.

LEADER GUIDE **SESSION 5**

SUPPLIES AND PREP

Craft foam, scissors, yarn or plastic lacing, hole punches, ruler, pencils, stickers, self-stick foam letters, markers

- Cut the craft foam into 5-inch squares (2 squares per child).
- Print "Reminders" (page 105). Copy 1 set for each child.

ENGAGE OPTION TWO: LISTEN UP! REMINDERS

- Distribute craft foam pieces and hole punches.
- Guide the children to place their two foam pieces on top of one another.
- Say: "Punch holes about ½-inch from the edge around three sides."
- Assist as needed.
- Continue: "Lace yarn through the holes to sew the foam pieces together."
- Assist as needed.
- Invite the children to decorate their holders.
- Say: "I want to test your memory. I will read aloud seven words. See how many of the words you can remember."
- Read aloud the following words: pray, trust, listen, wait, know, check, and follow.
- Invite the children to recall the words.
- Congratulate the children on remembering the words.
- Distribute "Reminders."
- Direct: "Cut apart your cards."
- Comment as the children cut apart the cards: "Let's talk about these actions and relate them to what we learned today."
- Read aloud Philippians 4:6.
- State: "We should pray about everything. As we pray, we should ask God to show us His plans for our lives."
- Read aloud Proverbs 3:5-6.
- Say: "We need to trust God hears our prayers and is working in our lives. We should trust His plans for us."
- Read aloud Job 42:4.
- Explain: "Instead of always talking to God, we should be still and listen to what He says."
- Read aloud Psalm 27:14.
- State: "God's timing is not always our timing. We should patiently wait for His answer to our requests."
- Read aloud Isaiah 41:20.
- Say: "God has a way of showing us His answers. We should watch for what God is doing."
- Read aloud 1 Thessalonians 5:21.
- State: "We should always check what we think is God's answer. We can check what we hear with what the Bible says. God will never tell us to do something that is not what the Bible says."
- Read aloud Matthew 4:19.
- Explain: "Once we know God's will, ask Him to help us follow His plan."
- Say: "Place your cards in your holders. This week, review your cards. Ask God to help you listen to Him and follow His plans for your life."
- Pray for each child to listen and respond to what God says to him.

ENGAGE OPTION THREE: MATCH THEM UP

- Call attention to the cards.
- Say: "We will use these cards to help us discover some people God spoke to. We will also discover how God spoke to these individuals."
- Assign each child, or groups of children, to a Scripture card.
- Explain: "Locate the verses in your Bible. Read and discover to whom God spoke. Locate the card with the name on it, but do not move it. Carefully unroll your party streamer and connect the Scripture card with the name card. Next, locate the card stating how God spoke to the person. Once again, unroll the party streamer and connect the cards. When everyone is finished, we will have a party-streamer spider web in the room."
- Assist the children in locating and reading the Bible verses.
- Ensure the party streamers stay attached to the wall.
- Summarize each Scripture passage by asking the children to state to whom and how God spoke.
- Select a volunteer to read aloud Jeremiah 29:11.
- Say: "God had a plan for the people we read about. Does God have a plan for us?"
- Continue: "God knows what is best for us. He wants us to follow His plans."
- Pray for each child to listen and respond to what God says.
- Say: "Look at the web we created. Let's see if we can move from one side of the room to the other without touching the party streamers."
- Allow the children to move through the web.

Ending The Lesson

- Ask: "What are some of the things you hear every day?"
- Invite responses.
- Say: "If we are not careful, we can become so busy we do not listen to God speaking to us. God wants to tell us what He wants us to do. Every day this week, make it a priority to spend time listening to God. Ask Him to show you the plans He has for you and then follow them."
- Share a brief testimony of how you listen to and follow God's plan for your life.
- Call attention to "Experiencing God at Home" in the *Experiencing God Kids Learner Guide* (page 12).
- Challenge the children to complete the activities at home.
- Invite the children to silently pray after you: "Dear God / Thank You for speaking to me. / Help me listen to what You say. / Help me follow the plans You have for my life. / Help me experience You every day. / Amen."

SUPPLIES AND PREP

Bibles, index cards, marker, masking tape, 8 rolls of party streamers

- Write the Scripture references, individuals, and summary statements of "Match It Up!" (page 4) on individual index cards.
- Randomly attach the Scripture cards to one wall leaving space around the cards. Attach the name cards in various locations around the room. Attach the summary cards on opposite walls from the name cards. Attach the end of 1 party streamer under each name card.
- Place tape loops near each card.

Session 6:
I MUST HAVE FAITH

Teacher Preparation

BIBLE PASSAGE
1 Samuel 16–17

BIBLE TRUTH
I must have faith and take action to follow God and join in His work.

LIFE APPLICATION
When God shows me something He wants me to do, I must believe He will help me and then do what He says in order to see Him use me.

KEY VERSE
1 Chronicles 28:20a

PRAYER CHALLENGE
Before beginning your planning, pray God will prepare your heart and work through you to speak to the children. Pray God will prepare the children to hear and apply what they learn so they can experience all He has planned for them.

- Read 1 Samuel 16–17. Place yourself in David's position as the events unfold.
- Read the life application statement (side column). First Samuel 16 does not state how long Samuel mourned for Saul, but God was ready for Samuel to move on. God instructed him to anoint the next king of Israel.
- Notice Samuel's actions in 16:6. He believed, based on human characteristics that Eliab (ih LIGH ab), Jesse's oldest son was the most "king-like" and therefore was God's chosen man. Read verse 7. God told Samuel that He judges differently than man. God does not look at the outward appearance, but the heart. As Jesse presented each of his sons, God told Samuel none of them were His chosen one.
- Reflect on the selection of David (verses 11-13). When David was presented, God affirmed to Samuel, David was the man He had chosen. At this point, God's Spirit came upon David.
- Review the events described in verses 14-23. David was skilled at playing the lyre. He had learned to defend his sheep against lions and bears. He attributed his ability to defeat lions and bears to God's protection (1 Samuel 17:34-37).
- Notice the situation between the Israelites and the Philistines. The Israelites were taunted to select a soldier to fight the Philistine's giant—Goliath. When David heard the way Goliath taunted the Israelites and their God, David became angry.
- Imagine reading the story of David and Goliath for the first time. At first, King Saul believed David was too young to fight a seasoned warrior like Goliath. David assured Saul that God would protect him. After being offered and declining Saul's own armor, David selected a sling and five stones. His greatest weaponry was his incredible faith in God.
- Compare and contrast Goliath's strength with David's. Goliath came with victories over people, David came with the strength of God. David knew God is more powerful than any sword or spear. David also knew that God's reputation, not his own, was at stake.
- Think about the events of David's life. Through these verses, we see David's trust in God's protection. David was presented with an opportunity to exercise his faith in God. David seized the opportunity. God used David to accomplish His purpose and to bring glory to His name.

- Think about the children in your ministry. What plans does God have for their lives? How are you equipping them to believe God will help them do what He says? How are you preparing them to accomplish His purposes and plans to bring glory to His name?

Getting Ready

- Greet each child by name.
- Distribute *Experiencing God Kids Learner Guide* and pencils.
- Guide the children to complete "Crack the Code" (page 1).
- Invite the children to discuss challenges they faced during the week.
- Ask: "How did you deal with these challenges?"

Excite (5-8 MINUTES)

- Ask: "How do you respond when someone asks you to do something you have never done or to do something scary? Do you do the action? Why or why not?"
- Display the box.
- Invite a volunteer to stand beside the box.
- Continue: "If I asked you to place your hand inside this box and tell me what you feel, would you do it? Why or why not?"
- Allow the volunteer to respond.
- Invite the child to reach in and feel the item.
- Say: "Describe what you feel."
- Guide the child to describe what he feels.
- Ask: "Was it easy to follow my directions? Do you think I would let you place your hand into a box that contained something that would harm you? Why?"
- Say: "I placed a bowl of grapes in the box. What if you did not know me, would you follow my directions? Why or why not?"
- Ask: "Can you think of one word to describe what you had to do for me?"
- Invite the children to shout out words describing actions.
- Explain: "The word I am looking for is *trust*. You can trust me to not let anything harmful happen to you. I want what is best for you. Can we say the same thing about God? Can we trust Him? Does He want what is the best for us?"

Examine (10 MINUTES)

- Inquire: "What did you discover in the 'Crack the Code'?"
- Select a volunteer to read aloud the "Crack the Code" message.
- Say: "In order to be a part of what God is doing, we have to take action and follow Him. That means we have to do something. To experience Him, we have to join Him in His work."

SUPPLIES AND PREP

Bibles, Session 6 *Experiencing God Kids Learner Guide* (1 per child), pencils, large box with lid, utility knife (adult use only), bowl of grapes, "Reality 1–5" posters (Insert), tape, slingshots, foam balls, laundry baskets, construction paper, index cards, red and blue markers, colored pencils

- Cut a hole in the side of the box large enough for a child to insert his hand.
- Place the bowl of grapes in the box.
- Display "Reality 1–4" posters.
- Write point values on individual sheets of construction paper and attach to the laundry baskets.
- Tape a "slingshot" line on the floor about 10 feet from the baskets.
- Alternate using red and blue markers to write the words of 1 Chronicles 28:20a on construction paper.

TIP

Place additional items in the box and allow volunteers to feel and identify.

CRACK THE CODE

I must have faith and take action to follow God and join in His work.

LEADER GUIDE **SESSION 6**

- Review the previous *Experiencing God* realities (Reality 1–4 posters).
- Invite the children to recall information related to the realities.
- Display "Reality 5" poster.
- Enlist a volunteer to read aloud the poster.
- Say: "Let's discover what this reality means and how it applies to our lives."

Explore (25 MINUTES)

SOUND EFFECTS
David—"I'll obey."
Goliath—Make muscle arms, say "Grr!"
Philistines—"Oh no!"
Israelites—"God is on our side."

- Explain: "I need your help as I tell the Bible story. I want you to make sound effects for the people."
- Describe and practice the "Sound Effects" (side margin).
- Open your Bible to 1 Samuel 16.
- Say: "Last week we learned how God called Samuel. Throughout his life, Samuel obeyed God. God instructed Samuel to anoint a man named Saul as the King of Israel. For a while, Saul did what God wanted him to do, however, over time Saul turned away from God. As a result of Saul's actions, God decided Saul would no longer be king. This is where the events in our Bible story today begin."
- Tell the Bible story in your own words.

TIP
Tell the Bible story without sound effects the first time.

DAVID TAKES ACTION

God spoke to Samuel asking, "How long will you be upset for Saul? I have rejected him as king. Go to Bethlehem, to the home of Jesse. I have selected one of his sons as the next king."

Samuel obeyed God. When he arrived at Jesse's home, Samuel saw Eliab (ih LIGH ab), Jesse's oldest son. Samuel felt Eliab was the man God wanted to become king. God said to Samuel, "Do not just look at the physical appearance. I do not want Eliab to become king. I can see things you cannot see."

One by one, Jesse introduced his sons to Samuel. Each time, God said to Samuel, "This is not the one." Finally, Samuel asked Jesse, "Do you have any more sons?" Jesse said, "I have my youngest son, but he is caring for the sheep." Samuel instructed Jesse to send for **David**. When **David** arrived, God said to Samuel, "This is the man I want you to anoint as king." In front of **David**'s brothers, Samuel took oil and poured it on **David** and anointed him king. From that day on, God's spirit took control of **David**.

Even though Samuel had anointed **David** as king, **David** did not immediately become king. Saul remained king. However, Saul had problems. God sent an evil spirit to torment (bother) Saul. Some of Saul's men suggested finding someone who could play the harp to help Saul feel better. One of Saul's servants knew **David** could play the harp. **David** was sent by his father to play the harp for Saul.

Israel was at war with the **Philistines**. The **Israelites** were on one side of the Valley of Elah [EE luh], the **Philistines** on the other. The champion of the **Philistines** was a man named **Goliath**. He stood 9 feet 9 inches tall. His bronze helmet and armor weighed 125 pounds. He had armor on his shins and a sword slung on his back. The point of his spear weighed 15 pounds. In front of **Goliath** was a man carrying a shield.

Goliath shouted to the **Israelites**, "Why do you line up prepared for battle? Pick one of your men to come fight me! If he wins, the **Philistines** will become your servants. If I win, you will become our servants." When Saul and his army heard **Goliath**'s words, they became afraid.

Three of **David**'s brothers were fighting in Saul's army. Jesse prepared food for **David** to take to his brothers. Early one morning, **David** reached the battle area. As he visited with his brothers, **Goliath** came out and shouted at the **Israelite** army. **Goliath** had done this every morning and evening for 40 days. **David** asked, "What will happen to the man who kills this **Philistine**?" As **David** listened to the men talk, Eliab, his oldest brother, became upset that **David** had come to the battle area.

David declared, "I will go fight this **Philistine**!" Saul replied, "You cannot fight this man. You are just a young man. This **Philistine** has been fighting since you were a young boy." **David** said, "As a shepherd, I fought lions and bears. This man will not be a problem for me. God saved me from lions and bears, He will save me from this man."

Saul agreed to let **David** fight **Goliath**. In fact, Saul had his own armor given to **David** for him to wear. After putting on the armor, **David** was unable to walk. **David** said, "I cannot use this armor. I am not used to it." **David** took the armor off. He took his staff in one hand and picked up five smooth stones from the brook and placed them in his bag. With his sling in hand, **David** walked toward **Goliath**.

Goliath and **David** approached one another. **Goliath** made fun of **David** because he was young, good-looking, and healthy. **Goliath** asked, "Am I a dog that you are fighting me with sticks?" Then **Goliath** cursed **David**.

David said to **Goliath**, "You have weapons to fight me with, but I am fighting you in the name of God. You have mistreated Him. Today, God will defeat you, and then everyone will know Israel has a God. Everyone will know He defeated you."

Goliath prepared to attack **David**. **David** ran to meet him. **David** took a stone and put it in his sling. He slung the sling and released the stone, hitting **Goliath** on his forehead. **Goliath** fell on his face to the ground. **David** used **Goliath**'s own sword to cut off his head. When the **Philistines** saw their champion was dead, they ran away. The **Israelites** chased after them.

REVIEW QUESTIONS

1. For whom was Samuel upset? **A: Saul**; B: Eli; C: David
2. Who was David's dad? A: Eliab; **B: Jesse**; C: Saul
3. Who did God tell Samuel to anoint as king? A: Eliab; B: Elah; **C: David**
4. True or **False**: David immediately became king.
5. What instrument did David play? A: flute; B: drum; **C: harp**
6. Who were the Israelites at war with? **A: Philistines**; B: Egyptians; C: Greeks
7. Who was the champion of the Philistines? A: Gad; **B: Goliath**; C: David
8. How tall was Goliath? A: 9 feet; **B: 9 feet 9 inches**; C: 9 feet 11 inches
9. True or **False**: Eliab was excited about David fighting Goliath.
10. Who gave David his armor to wear? A: Samuel; **B: Saul**; C: Eliab
11. How many stones did David pick up? A: 1; B: 3; **C: 5**
12. In whose name did David say he would defeat Goliath? A: Saul's; B: Jesse's; **C: God's**
13. Where did the stone hit Goliath? A: chest; B: elbow; **C: forehead**
14. What did the Philistines do when they saw Goliath was dead? A: **ran away**; B: worshiped God; C: cried

LEADER GUIDE SESSION 6

- Ask: "How do you think David responded when Samuel anointed him king? How do you think David's brothers responded? If you were David, would you have volunteered to fight Goliath? Why or why not?"
- Read aloud "Reality 5" poster.
- Continue: "Do you think David believed God wanted him to fight Goliath? In what ways did God use David?"
- Distribute colored pencils.
- Guide the children to complete "Be the Artist" (pages 2-3).
- Encourage the children to compare their drawings with one another.
- Continue: "Let's review what we learned today. I will ask your team a question. If you answer correctly, you may use the sling to shoot a ball at a basket. Your team earns the number of points on the basket the ball lands in. If the ball does not land in a basket, you receive no points."
- Form three teams.
- Distribute index cards and markers to each team.
- Say: "I will ask you a multiple choice or true/false question. Write down the correct answer. Do not show me until I instruct you to do so."
- Read aloud the first "Review Questions" (page 53).
- Guide each team to write down an answer.
- Invite the teams to reveal the answers.
- Allow one person from each correctly answering team to stand behind the tape line and shoot the ball.
- Award points.
- Continue as time allows.
- Ask: "How did David's faith and trust in God make a difference in his life?"
- State: "Our actions and attitudes show what we believe about God. When we face challenges, we can trust God to help us through them. What are some challenges kids your age face?"
- Talk about challenges children face.
- Say: "The Bible can help us know how to deal with these challenges."
- Guide the children to complete "Follow God's Instructions" (page 4).
- Read aloud the statements and Bible verses.
- Say: "Let's ask God to help us apply these verses to our lives."
- Pray, asking God to help the children apply the concepts presented in these verses to their lives. Thank God for His promises and the assurance He will keep them.
- Say: "Throughout his life, David showed he trusted and followed God. David was not perfect, he made many mistakes. His sins impacted his relationship with God, but God still loved and used him. Let's read some words David said to his son, Solomon. Open your Bible to 1 Chronicles 28:20a."
- Assist as needed.
- Select a volunteer to read aloud the verse.
- Ask: "If you were Solomon, how would you feel hearing your father say these words to you? Do you think Solomon saw David living out his belief and trust in God?"

FOLLOW GOD'S INSTRUCTIONS

- **Romans 8:28**—"I am not discouraged ..."
- **Philippians 4:13**—"I can face a difficult ..."
- **Philippians 4:6**—"Every time I begin ..."
- **Matthew 6:14-15**—"I forgive someone ..."
- **1 Peter 5:7**—"I talk with God ..."

TIP
Assist children in locating the verse in their Bibles.

GOD IS ALWAYS AT WORK AROUND ME.

LEADER GUIDE **REALITY POSTER 1**

GOD WANTS A PERSONAL RELATIONSHIP WITH ME.

LEADER GUIDE **REALITY POSTER 2**

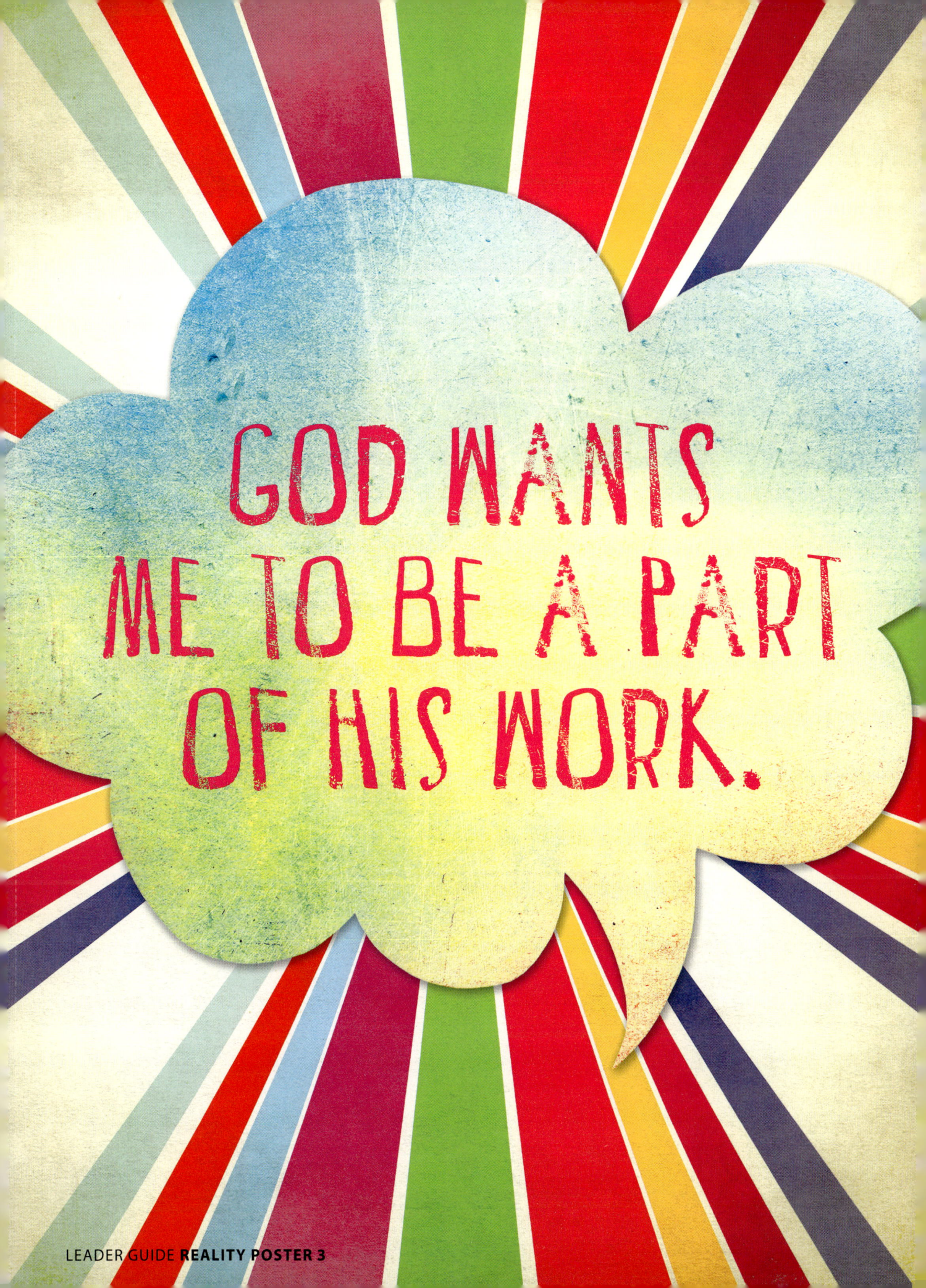

GOD WANTS ME TO BE A PART OF HIS WORK.

LEADER GUIDE **REALITY POSTER 3**

GOD SPEAKS AND SHOWS ME WHAT HE WANTS ME TO DO.

LEADER GUIDE **REALITY POSTER 4**

I MUST HAVE FAITH AND TAKE ACTION TO FOLLOW GOD AND JOIN IN HIS WORK.

LEADER GUIDE **REALITY POSTER 5**

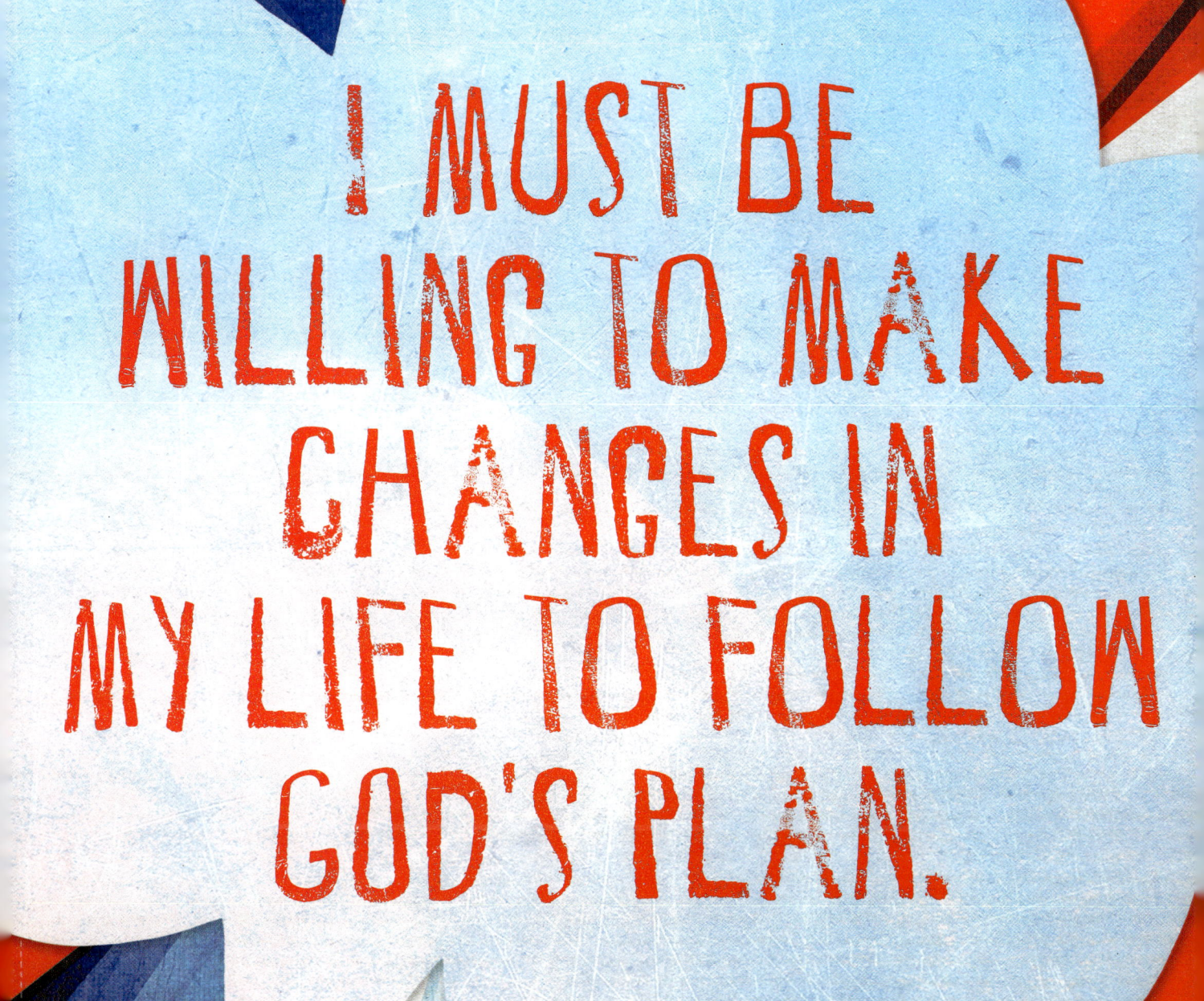

I MUST BE WILLING TO MAKE CHANGES IN MY LIFE TO FOLLOW GOD'S PLAN.

I KNOW AND EXPERIENCE GOD WHEN I OBEY HIM.

LEADER GUIDE **REALITY POSTER 7**

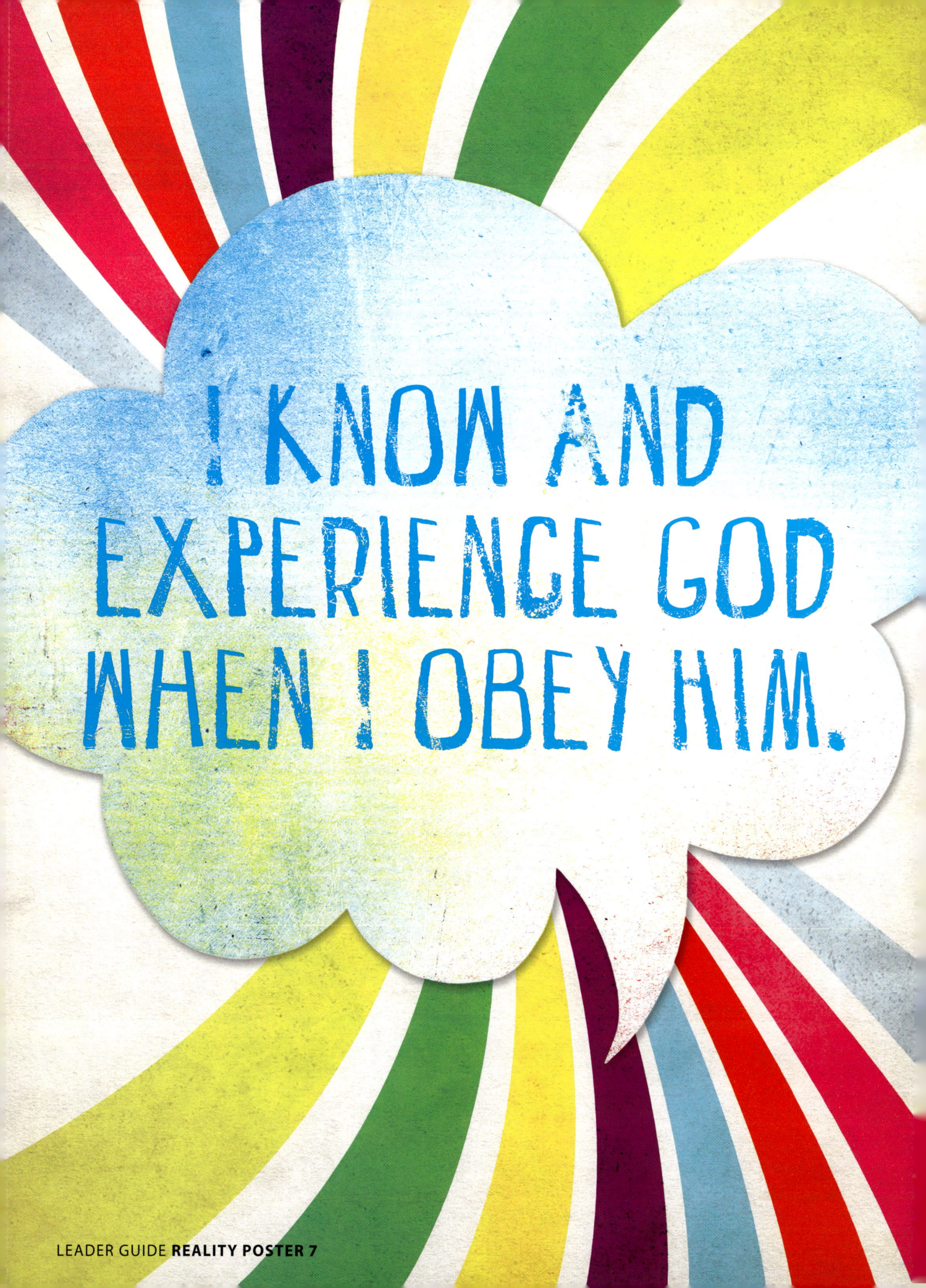

You had a problem and asked God to help you know what to do.	God gave you an idea or thought (wisdom) that helped you solve or get through the problem.
You asked God to let you be a part of His work.	You were asked to help in a new ministry at church where you were challenged to tell someone about Jesus.
You were upset and asked God to help you calm down.	As you thought about God, His peace made you feel better and helped you trust Him more.
For several months you prayed about something specific. You trusted God would take care of the situation for you. You began to feel God was not listening to you.	Just about the time you were ready to give up praying, something happened and you knew God answered your prayer.
You asked God to help you love your family and friends better.	During a difficult time with your family and friends, you felt God telling to you stop arguing, calm down, and listen. God helped you to love your family and friends.
You asked God to help you listen well at school, study hard, and do well.	You started enjoying school, studied more, and made better grades.
You asked God to help you be more respectful to your parents.	You noticed you are more obedient, helpful, and cooperative at home.
You asked God to help you get along with a kid who picks on you.	You got the courage to talk with the kid and discovered he really wanted someone to be his friend.
You prayed one of your friends would ask Jesus to be his Savior and Lord.	Your friend asked you how he could ask Jesus to be his Savior and Lord.
Someone asked you why you believe in Jesus. You asked God to know what to say.	As you started to speak, you knew exactly what to say to the person about why you believe in Jesus.
A friend asked you what she should do in a specific situation. You silently asked God to tell you what to say.	You knew exactly what to tell your friend. The advice you shared is what God told you to say.
Someone asked for prayer but did not tell you about his prayer request.	You prayed for the person, saying something like, "God, You know what this person needs. Please meet her needs."

LEADER GUIDE **PRAYER AND SOLUTION**

YOU MAKE PEOPLE LAUGH AND HAPPY.	YOU ARE A NICE PERSON.
YOU ARE A GOOD FRIEND TO OTHERS.	YOU ARE A KIND AND GENTLE PERSON.
YOU ARE VERY TALENTED.	YOU ARE A GOOD LEADER.
YOU ARE LIKABLE.	YOU ARE A GOOD LISTENER.
YOU MAKE OTHERS FEEL LOVED.	YOU ARE FRIENDLY.
YOU HAVE A GOOD SENSE OF HUMOR.	YOU ARE FUN TO BE WITH.
YOU ARE A HELPFUL PERSON.	I THINK THAT YOU ARE GREAT.
YOU ARE SMART.	I'M GLAD THAT YOU ARE MY FRIEND.

LEADER GUIDE **BLESSING STRIPS**

Find someone who needs cheering up. Tell her three things you think are great about her.

Encourage the teacher by telling her what you like about this class.

Say nice things to at least three people in the class.

Ask the teacher how you can help her—then do what she says.

Ask the teacher how you can help clean up—then do what she says.

Find a quiet place to sit. Close your eyes and silently pray for two of your friends.

Find a quiet place to sit. Close your eyes and silently pray for your teachers.

Find a Bible. Locate Matthew 6:31. Tell three people what you learned.

Get a piece of paper. Write and deliver an encouraging note to someone.

Get a piece of paper. Write and deliver an encouraging note to your teacher.

Find a quiet place to sit. Close your eyes and silently ask God to give you wisdom about how you can join Him in what He is doing.

LEADER GUIDE **STATEMENTS**

- Demonstrate the sign language in "Actions to Remember" (page 5).
- Display "1 Chronicles 28:20a" poster.
- Say: "Let's say the verse in different sections. Girls, stand, and say the words in red and do the sign language. Boys, stand and say the words in blue and do the sign language. Sit down when you are not speaking."
- Guide the children to take turns standing and saying the verse.
- Challenge the children to apply the verse to their lives.

Engage (20 MINUTES)

ENGAGE OPTION ONE: FOLLOWING INSTRUCTIONS

- Ask: "Do you like to follow instructions? What are some instructions you do not like to follow? Why don't you like these instructions?"
- Continue: "What are some instructions you like to follow? Why is it easier to follow these instructions?"
- Explain: "Let's play a game to test how well you follow instructions."
- Say: "I will give you a sheet with a list of instructions on it. Read all of the instructions carefully. The first person to complete the sheet will receive a special prize."
- Distribute "Follow Instructions."
- Observe as the children complete the activity.
- Reward prizes.
- Ask: "Was it easy to follow these instructions? How did you feel when you saw someone doing an activity she did not need to do? What did you learn about following instructions from this game?"
- Distribute a snack to each child.
- Distribute *Experiencing God Kids Learner Guides* and pencils.
- Guide the children to complete "What Does God Want Me to Do?" (pages 10-11).
- Ask: "What does God want us to do? Can you honestly tell God you are willing to do whatever He asks you to do? If you are scared—tell God. If you are excited—tell God. If you are ready—tell God. No matter how you feel—tell God."
- Provide quiet time for the children to reflect and to pray.

SUPPLIES AND PREP
Bibles, Session 6 *Experiencing God Kids Learner Guide* (1 per child), pencils, snack, prizes
- Copy "Follow Instructions" (page 106) (1 per child).

TIPS
- Allow each child to work with a partner.
- Pair non-readers with readers.

ENGAGE OPTION TWO: BIBLE HERO POSTERS

- Distribute index cards and pencils.
- Ask: "Other than God or Jesus, who do you think is the greatest Bible hero? Write the person's name on your card."
- Assist with spelling and writing.
- Gather the cards.
- Read aloud each name, inviting the children to review the person's life, his response to God's calling, what he did, and how he is remembered.
- Select a volunteer to read aloud Luke 16:10.
- Ask: "How does this verse apply to the people we discussed?"

SUPPLIES AND PREP
Bibles, poster board, markers, items to decorate posters, index cards, pencils

LEADER GUIDE **SESSION 6**

BIBLE HERO SUGGESTIONS

Noah, Abraham, Joseph, Moses, Joshua, Gideon, Samson, Deborah, David, Samuel, Solomon, Elijah, Esther, Ruth, Nehemiah, Daniel, Peter, John the Baptist, Paul

TIP

Display the posters in the hallway for parents to see.

SUPPLIES AND PREP

Newspaper, Session 6 *Experiencing God Kids Learner Guide* (1 per child), pencils, large sheets of paper, markers, plastic bags (1 per child), tape

- Secure the paper to the wall.

- Say: "Let's make posters about some of these people. You can work with a friend or by yourself. Pick a person we talked about. Design a poster to help other people know how this person took action to follow God and join in His work."
- Distribute poster board, markers, and other craft supplies.
- Assist the children in designing posters.
- Say: "Do we have heroes we can follow today? We can all be heroes by listening and doing what God tells us to do."
- Distribute *Experiencing God Kids Learner Guides* and pencils.
- Guide the children to complete "What Does God Want Me to Do?" (pages 10-11).
- Ask: "What does God want us to do? Can you honestly tell God you are willing to do whatever He asks you to do? If you are scared—tell God. If you are excited—tell God. If you are ready—tell God. No matter how you feel—tell God."
- Provide quiet time for the children to reflect and pray.

ENGAGE OPTION THREE: FACING MY GIANTS

- Distribute several sheets of newspaper to each child.
- Instruct: "Crumple your newspaper into small balls, the tighter the better."
- Ask: "What are some 'giants' (difficult things) we face in our lives?"
- Write the "giants" children face on large sheets of paper.
- Ask: "Do you ever feel like there is nothing you can do to face these giants? How do you stand up to these giants?"
- Discuss ways children can stand up to the obstacles they face.
- Say: "David defeated his 'giant.' God guided the stone to hit Goliath on the forehead. David defeated Goliath by trusting in God. Many of the people we read about in the Bible depended on their faith in God to defeat their 'giants.' Think about how these people demonstrated faith in God: Noah, Abraham, Esther, Daniel, Peter, Paul, Stephen, and Zacchaeus."
- Continue: "People who have faith and take action to follow God and join Him in His work can know they will defeat their 'giants.'"
- Call attention to the "giants" kids face.
- Say: "Let's pretend we are David. These 'stones' (paper balls) represent the stone David used to defeat Goliath. Let's toss these 'stones' at the 'giants' we face."
- Guide the children to throw the crumbled paper at the items.
- Gather the children together.
- Distribute *Experiencing God Kids Learner Guides* and pencils.
- Guide the children to complete "What Does God Want Me to Do?" (pages 10-11).
- Ask: "What does God want us to do? Can you honestly tell God you are willing to do whatever He asks you to do? If you are scared—tell God. If you are excited—tell God. If you are ready—tell God. No matter how you feel—tell God."
- Provide quiet time for the children to reflect and pray.
- Distribute plastic bags.
- Say: "If you would like to take some crumpled papers home to remind you to trust God, you may."
- Allow the children to gather crumpled paper and place in the bags.

Ending the Session

- Ask: "What did you learn today that will make a difference in your life?"
- Continue: "When you face a 'giant' who tests your trust in God, what will you do?"
- Invite the children to share how they can stand up to their "giants."
- Say: "This week, remember the words David said to his son, Solomon. Let's say the words of 1 Chronicles 28:20a as we do the sign language."
- Say and sign the verse.
- Explain: "I want to give you something to carry with you this week."
- Distribute stones.
- Say: "Place your stone in your pocket. When you face a difficult challenge this week, hold your stone in your hand and pray. Ask God to help you have faith and follow His instructions."
- Call attention to "Experiencing God at Home" in the *Experiencing God Kids Learner Guide* (page 12).
- Challenge the children to complete the activities at home.
- Invite the children to pray sentence prayers.
- Close the session in prayer.

SUPPLIES AND PREP
Small, smooth stones
(1 per child)

Session 7:
ADJUSTING TO GOD'S PLAN

Teacher Preparation

BIBLE PASSAGE
2 Kings 5:1-16

BIBLE TRUTH
I must be willing to make changes in my life to follow God's plan.

LIFE APPLICATION
When I understand God's truth and what He is saying to me, I must be willing to change my attitudes and actions to follow His plan.

KEY VERSE
Matthew 6:33

PRAYER CHALLENGE
Before beginning your planning, pray God will prepare your heart and work through you to speak to the children. Pray God will prepare the children to hear and apply what they learn so they can experience all He has planned for them.

- Read 2 Kings 5:1-16. How would you describe Naaman (NAY uh muhn)?
- Think about the spiritual conditions in Israel. Due to King Jehoram (jih HOH ruhm) and the Israelites' disobedience, God allowed other nations to defeat them. One such nation was Syria, located north of Israel.
- Reflect on Naaman's actions and attitude. He was a well-respected, successful Syrian military commander. However, he had a medical condition—leprosy. For Hebrews, leprosy rendered a person ceremonially unclean. As a result, individuals with leprosy were isolated from the rest of the community. This did not seem to be the case in Syria.
- Reread verses 2-3. The girl was taken from her home by Naaman's army. Though nothing is stated about her family or what happened to them, we know she now served her enemies and possibly the very man responsible for her capture. Despite being a servant, she had concern for Naaman. Rather than allow Naaman to suffer, she suggested a way for him to be healed.
- Notice the servant girl knew about Elisha and how God worked through him to heal people. In suggesting Naaman go to Elisha, the girl displayed faith that God would extend grace and healing to non-Israelites—showing God had care and concern for all people.
- Reread 4-6. Naaman received permission from the King of Syria to go to Israel.
- Notice King Jehoram's reaction. He was upset. He knew he did not have the power to heal Naaman. King Jehoram suspected the Syrians wanted to provoke the Israelites.
- Observe Naaman's reaction. He was offended Elisha, the prophet, did not personally touch, and heal Naaman. He left in a great rage at being slighted.
- Reread verse 13-16. Naaman's servants listened and persuaded him to try Elisha's suggestion. Through Naaman's healing, God received the glory. Naaman acknowledged before all his men and Elisha that the God of Israel was the one and only true God.
- Reflect on the actions of the servant girl. She demonstrated great faith and was willing to love her enemies. Because of her actions and attitude, God was glorified and a foreign enemy received grace. As a result, Naaman acknowledged the one true God. God used the servant girl to change Naaman.

- Ask God to help you change your attitude and actions so you can be used by Him. Your response to difficult circumstances can have a great impact on people around you.

Getting Ready

- Greet each child by name.
- Distribute index cards and pencils.
- Guide each child to write his name on an index card.
- Gather cards (use in *Explore*).
- Distribute *Experiencing God Kids Learner Guide*.
- Guide the children to complete "Crack the Code" (page 1).

Excite (5-8 MINUTES)

- Say: "The Israelites were God's chosen people. He wanted to be their leader and for the people to always follow Him. However, the people wanted a king like the nations around them. God gave the people what they wanted. Some of Israel's kings and queens obeyed God. They led the people to keep God first. Other kings and queens did not serve God. They did not obey Him or follow His commands. Let's discover some of the people who served as kings and queens of Israel."
- Call attention to the cups.
- Explain: "Some of the cups have Bible verse references attached to them. Pick a cup and locate the verse in your Bible. Read the verse and discover the name of the king. Find the cup with the king's name on it. Place the cups—bottom to bottom, or top to top, on one other. See how tall of a structure you can make before the cups fall over."
- Assist the children in locating the verses, cups, and building a structure.
- Continue as time permits.

Examine (10 MINUTES)

- Inquire: "Did you enjoy stacking the cups? How did you feel when the cups fell over?"
- Comment: "Our attitudes and actions play a large part in how we do something. If we have bad attitudes, our actions show it. Let's see how quickly we can adjust our attitudes and actions."
- Continue: "Everyone stand up. I will call out an action for you to complete or an attitude to demonstrate. For example if I say, 'happy attitude' show me what a happy attitude looks like. Follow my directions as quickly as possible."

SUPPLIES AND PREP

Bibles, Session 7 *Experiencing God Kids Learner Guide* (1 per child); index cards; 24 plastic cups; tape; scissors; "Reality 6" poster (Insert), table, child-size Bible times clothes, GPS, 2 tap lights with batteries, 3 colors of sticky notes, marker, construction paper, pencils

- Print and cut apart "Kings" (page 103). Tape 1 strip to each cup. Mix the cups together and place on the table.
- Enlist 1 girl and 2 boys to act out the Bible story.
- Write the words of Matthew 6:33 on the construction paper.
- Write the words of Matthew 6:33 on individual sticky notes (make 3 complete color sets, 1 word per note). Attach in random order on a side wall.

CRACK THE CODE
I must be willing to change my attitudes and actions to follow God's plan.

- Call out various actions *(stand on one foot, shake hands with friends, turn around 3 times, do 10 jumping jacks, sing the ABCs, run in place, sit down then jump up, fist-bump someone, play air guitar, etc.)* and attitudes *(happy, mad, sad, surprised, carefree, disappointed, I don't care, etc.)*.
- Play as time permits.
- Summarize the attitudes and actions observed during the game.
- Ask: "What message did you discover in 'Crack the Code'?"
- Select a volunteer to read aloud the "Crack the Code" message.
- Inquire: "Do you have any actions or attitudes that need to change? If so, tell God. Ask Him to help you change so you can follow His plans."
- Pause as the children pray.
- Close the prayer time. Ask God to help everyone examine his attitudes and actions.

Explore (25 MINUTES)

- Display the GPS device.
- Ask: "Can someone tell me what this is and what it does?"
- Select a volunteer to explain what a GPS is and does.
- Say: "GPS stands for *global positioning system*. A GPS can find where you are located and tell you how to get to another location. In order for a GPS to work properly, you must follow the instructions. If the GPS says 'turn right,' you should turn right. What happens when you do not follow the GPS' instructions?"
- Invite the children to respond.
- Continue: "Many times the GPS will say 'recalculating' or it may say, 'When possible, make a U-turn.'"
- Display a Bible.
- Say: "This 'GPS' can help us follow God's plans. When we obey His plans, we go where He wants us to go. When we do not follow God's plans, we have to 'recalculate' or 'make a U-turn.'"
- Say: "We will learn about a man who had to adjust his attitudes and actions. We will also learn about a girl who had a good attitude and how her actions helped people know about God."
- Explain: "Today we have a special news report. Let's watch as Addy Actions interviews these individuals."

TIP
Remove the index cards with the actors' names.

NAAMAN LEARNS A LESSON

Addy: My name is Addy Actions and I'm reporting to you from the scene of a most amazing situation. Allow me to introduce the commander of the king of Aram's army, Naaman. *[to Naaman]* I've heard you described as a great man, a highly respected man, and a man through whom God allowed the Israelites to be defeated.

Naaman: That is how some people have described me.

Addy: I understand you had a skin disease.

Naaman: Yes, I had a disease called *leprosy*.

Addy: *[turn to girl]* I understand you were brought from the land of Israel to serve Naaman's wife.

Girl: That is true. During the battle between Syria and Israel, I was taken from my family and made to become a servant to Naaman's wife.

Addy: Tell me what happened after this.

Girl: I noticed sores on Naaman's body. I told his wife, "If Naaman would go to the prophet living in Samaria, he would heal him."

Addy: *[to Naaman]* Did you do what she said?

Naaman: I told the king of Aram what the girl said. The king told me to do what she suggested. He even gave me a letter to take to the king of Israel asking Elisha to cure me. I took 750 pounds of silver, 150 pounds of gold, and 10 changes of clothes with me.

Addy: What happened when you reached the king of Israel?

Naaman: The king was not happy. He tore his clothes and asked me, "Am I God? Do you expect me to heal you? You want to start a fight with me."

Addy: What happened next?

Naaman: Elisha, the man of God, heard the king was upset. He sent a letter to the king instructing me to go to him. I took my horses and chariots and went to Elisha.

Addy: Let me guess, Elisha came out, touched you, and made you well.

TIP
Suggest the children practice the drama before the session.

REVIEW QUESTIONS

1. How did people describe Naaman? *(great man, highly respected, God defeated the Israelites through him)*
2. What physical problem did Naaman have? *(skin disease—leprosy)*
3. What job did the young girl have? *(servant to Naaman's wife)*
4. Whom did the servant girl say Naaman should see? *(the prophet living in Samaria, Elisha)*
5. What did Naaman take with him on his trip? *(letter from the king of Aram, 750 pounds of silver, 150 pounds of gold, 10 changes of clothes)*
6. Was the king of Israel happy when Naaman told him what he wanted? *(no)*
7. What did Elisha tell Naaman to do? *(wash 7 times in the Jordan River)*
8. How did Naaman feel when he heard Elisha's instructions? *(mad)*
9. What did Naaman think Elisha would do? *(stand in front on him, call on God, wave his hand over him, and cure him)*
10. What happened when Naaman finally obeyed Elisha's instructions? *(He was healed.)*
11. What can we learn from the servant girl? *(Answers will vary.)*
12. What can we learn from Naaman? *(Answers will vary.)*

Naaman: No. In fact, I did not even see Elisha. He sent his messenger to tell me to go and wash seven times in the Jordan River. He said I would be clean and no longer have leprosy.

Addy: Did you obey his instructions?

Naaman: At first, I was so angry. I thought, *This man will stand in front of me and call on the name of his God. He will wave his hand over me and I will be cured.*

Addy: But that did not happen.

Naaman: No! I thought the rivers of Damascus were better for bathing than the Jordan. I could have washed in those rivers. Extremely upset, I turned around and left.

Addy: But you seem to be healed. What happened?

Naaman: My servants said to me, "If the prophet had told you to do something great, you would have done it. He simply told you to wash yourself in the Jordan River and you would be clean." Finally, I went to the Jordan River and washed myself seven times. The sores on my skin went away and my health was restored.

Addy: That must have been an amazing feeling.

Naaman: It was. I went back to the man of God, stood in front of him, and said, "I now know there is only one God in the whole world and He is the God of Israel."

Addy: What an amazing story of healing!

[Actors return to their seats.]

- Say: "I hope you listened carefully to our Bible story. I am going to select some of you to play 'What Do You Remember?'"
- Place the tap lights on the table.
- Display the index cards.
- Continue: "I will select two cards. The people whose names I pick will come stand behind the lights. I will read aloud a question. The first person to turn on his light by tapping it will get to answer the question."
- Select two cards and read aloud the names.
- Guide the children to stand behind the table.
- Demonstrate how to turn on the lights.
- Read aloud one of the "Review Questions" (side margin).
- Reveal the correct answer.
- Continue selecting cards and changing players as time permits.
- Say: "Let me tell you some things I observed during the game."
- Comment on actions and attitudes observed during the game.

- Display "Reality 6" poster.
- Select a volunteer to read aloud the poster.
- Ask: "How did the servant girl's attitude and actions affect her concern for Naaman? What can we learn from this girl?"
- Continue: "How did Naaman's attitude and actions almost keep him from being healed? What can we learn from Naaman?"
- Invite the children to discuss what they learned.
- Guide the children to complete "Attitude Checkup" (page 4) and "Attitude and Actions" (page 6-7).
- Read aloud the statements. Discuss which ones are ways to follow God's plan.
- Say: "Let's listen to two stories. As you listen, see if you can figure out how the people's attitudes and actions changed."
- Enlist volunteers to read aloud "Liam's Story" and "Carrie's Story" (pages 2-3).
- Talk about the attitudes and actions displayed in the story.
- Say: "We should have the same type of attitude as Jesus. Let's discover something Jesus told the people. Open your Bible to Matthew 6:33."
- Assist as needed.
- Enlist a volunteer to read aloud the verse.
- Display the verse poster.
- State: "Let's play a game with the words of Matthew 6:33."
- Guide the children to form three teams.
- Call attention to the sticky note words.
- Assign each team a sticky note color.
- Say: "When I say 'begin,' the first person on your team will run and locate the first word of the verse on the color of sticky note assigned to your team. Bring back the sticky note and place it on the floor in front of you. The next person will locate and bring back the second word. Remember to only get the color assigned to your team. Continue until you get all the words in order."
- Allow the children to retrieve the words.
- Say: "Let's read the verse aloud together."
- Read aloud the verse.
- Ask: "What did Jesus say we should seek? Why is it important to seek God's will? How will following God's will affect our attitudes and actions? What will happen when we obey this verse?"
- Challenge the children to memorize and apply the verse to their lives.
- Say: "We can be like Naaman and become upset and decide not to do what we are told, or we can listen to wisdom. If Naaman had not listened to his servants, he may not have been healed. His attitude and actions almost kept him from following God's plans."
- Guide the children to stand with their Bible verse teams.
- Say: "Form a circle with your feet touching the person standing beside you. Think about all the places the people beside you will go this week. Pray God will help the people have positive attitudes and actions."
- Pause while the children pray.
- Close the prayer time.

LEADER GUIDE SESSION 7

Engage (20 MINUTES)

SUPPLIES AND PREP
Index cards, markers, stopwatch, paper
- Write a profession on each card (1 per card): *bus driver, school teacher, doctor, librarian, missionary, construction worker, pilot,* and so forth.
- Invite a guest to share how she follows God's plans in her career.

TIP
Provide props related to the professions.

SUPPLIES AND PREP
4 containers, scissors, table tennis balls (3 per team), marker, table, tape, index cards
- Print "Choices" (page 101).
- Mark the balls so teams can identify theirs.
- Place the containers in the middle of the table.
- Write *Servant Girl, Naaman, Elisha,* and *King of Aram* on the cards (1 name per card).
- Tape a name card in front of each container.
- Invite a guest to share how she follows God's plans in her career.

ENGAGE OPTION ONE: GUESS MY JOB
- Form two teams.
- Explain: "Let's play 'Guess My Job.' One person from your team will select a card with a job printed on it. The person will act out the job for his team. If his team can guess what job he is acting out in 30 seconds or less, the team earns 1,000 points. If you do not correctly guess, the other team can guess for 500 points."
- Select a team to begin.
- Guide a team member to select a card and act out the profession.
- Call time at the end of 30 seconds.
- Record points.
- Change teams and continue as time permits.
- Display all the profession cards face up.
- Ask: "Which job do you think is the most difficult? Why?"
- Allow the children to rank the jobs from easiest to most difficult.
- Continue: "What type of training is needed to have the most difficult job?"
- Discuss the work and effort (education, preparation, training, equipment, practices, costs) for the job.
- Emphasis: "These jobs require a lot of work and preparation. They also require the people to have good attitudes. How would you feel if a firefighter came to your house but had a bad attitude about helping you? What would you do if he said, 'I know I'm a firefighter, but I don't feel like helping today?'"
- Say: "You may already know what type of job you want when you grow up. You can begin learning about the job now, but you most likely cannot do much more to prepare right now. We all have something we can do now—we can learn how to follow God's plans for our lives. God wants us to join Him where He is working. Let's listen to how someone serves God in her job."
- Invite the guest to share how she follows God's plans for her in her career.
- Allow the children to ask the guest questions.
- Thank the guest.
- Pray for each child by name.

ENGAGE OPTION TWO: SMALL CHOICES, BIG RESULTS
- Ask: "What is the most important decision you made today? What about this week? How did your decision impact your life?"
- Invite the children to respond.
- Form teams of five or six children.
- Call attention to the containers.
- Say: "I will read aloud a statement about a person. One person on each team will bounce a table tennis ball on the table and get it to land in the container of the person's name I described. The first team to get a ball into the correct container will earn 1,000 points."
- Guide each team to select a player.
- Distribute table tennis balls.

- Read aloud the corresponding statement related to one of the name tags.
- Invite the children to bounce the balls until one lands in the correct container.
- Award points.
- Select new players from each team and continue.
- Review the choices the individuals made.
- Ask: "How did their choices impact their lives? How did these people choose to follow God's plans? Do you think there were times these individuals had to change their attitudes and actions?"
- Talk about the people's attitudes and actions.
- Explain: "These people made choices to follow God's plans. God wants us to join Him where He is working. Let's listen to how someone serves God in her job."
- Invite the guest to share how she follows God's plans for her in her career.
- Allow the children to ask the guest questions.
- Thank the guest.
- Pray for each child by name.

ENGAGE OPTION THREE: MAKING ADJUSTMENTS

- Place the clay and tub of water on the table.
- Ask: "Do you think this clay will float? Why or why not?"
- Place the clay in the water.
- Guide the children to observe what happens.
- Inquire: "How could we change the clay to make it float?"
- Allow the children to discuss options.
- Direct the children to mold the clay into various shapes until it floats (roll the clay into a flat, pancake shape).
- Congratulate the children on their efforts.
- Display the coins.
- Ask: "How many coins do you think we can place on the clay until it sinks?" Invite the children to make suggestions.
- Place coins, one at a time, on the clay until it sinks.
- Test different shapes of clay to see which holds the most coins.
- Ask: "Why did changing the clay's shape make it float? How did the coins affect the clay's ability to float?"
- Say: "Imagine the clay could talk and said, 'I don't want to be changed. I want to remain a lump.' Would it have floated? What if the clay had said, 'Stop putting coins on me!' Would we have been able to discover how many coins we could make float?"
- Continue: "In order to accomplish our plan, we needed to change the clay. We can learn an important lesson from this experiment. In order for God to use us, we have to be willing to change. If we are not willing to change, God cannot use us the way He wants. We will miss what He wants to do through us."
- State: "Let's listen to how someone served God in her job."
- Invite the guest to share how she follows God's plans for her in her career.
- Allow the children to ask the guest questions.
- Thank the guest.
- Pray for each child by name.

SUPPLIES AND PREP
Fist-size lump of clay, plastic storage tub, water, coins, towels, table
- Fill the container about halfway full with water.
- Invite a guest to share how she follows God's plans in her career.

TIP
Practice the activity at home.

Ending the Session

- Ask: "Does anyone need an attitude check? Are you willing to change your attitude and actions so you can be a part of God's plans for your life?"
- Challenge: "This week when things do not go the way you want, ask yourself, 'Is God helping me adjust my attitude? If so, what should I do?'"
- Guide everyone to find a partner.
- Say: "Stand facing your partner. Point to your partner and tell him 'Only you can change your attitude! Only you can change your actions!'"
- Direct the children to say the statements several times.
- Continue: "When I say 'change,' find a new partner and tell her the same thing."
- Call out "change" several times, allowing the children to find new partners.
- Ask: "Who can change my attitude? Who can change my actions?"
- Say: "We are responsible for our own attitudes and actions. When we have the right attitudes and commit to do the right actions, we are ready for God to use."
- Call attention to "Experiencing God at Home" in the *Experiencing God Kids Learner Guide* (page 12).
- Challenge the children to complete the activities at home.
- Close the session in prayer.

WHAT CHANGES DO YOU NEED TO MAKE IN YOUR LIFE?

LEADER GUIDE **SESSION 7**

SESSION 7

67

Session 8: EXPERIENCING GOD

Teacher Preparation

BIBLE PASSAGE
Daniel 1 and 3

BIBLE TRUTH
I experience God and know Him better when I obey Him and do what He says.

LIFE APPLICATION
When God speaks and I obey Him, I will learn more about God and experience His power in my life.

KEY VERSE
John 14:23

PRAYER CHALLENGE
Before beginning your planning, pray God will prepare your heart and work through you to speak to the children. Pray God will prepare the children to hear and apply what they learn so they can experience all He has planned for them.

- Read Daniel 1:1-7. In 605 B.C., King Nebuchadnezzar (neb yoo kad NEZ uhr) of Babylon conquered Jerusalem. This period is known as "The Babylonian Exile," a time of judgment for Israel's continued disobedience. Notice the items the king took with him back to Babylon—sacred items from Israel's treasury as well as some of Israel's brightest young men including Daniel, Hananiah (HAN uh NIGH uh), Mishael (MISH eh uhl), and Azariah (az uh RIGH uh). The men were trained in Babylonian culture, language, and literature as well as given names that referred to Babylonian gods. The king sought to cut off these men from their own culture and religious identity, thus making them useful servants of Babylon.
- Read Daniel 1:8-16. Reflect on the courage of the exiles. These men were only teenagers, but were resolved to stay loyal to God and their Jewish heritage.
- Read Daniel 1:17-20. What was the result of these teenagers' faithfulness to God?
- Read Daniel 3:1-6. At the height of his empire, Nebuchadnezzar proudly erected a golden statue. At the dedication of the statue, all the leading officials of the empire gathered together. At the sound of the music, everyone was to bow and worship the image. The result of disobedience was the fiery furnace.
- Read Daniel 3:7-23. How did the king learn about Shadrach (SHAD rak), Meshach (MEE shak), and Abednego's (uh BED-nih goh) refusal to obey his order? Notice the men's commitment. They were loyal to God and confident He would save them from the heat of the furnace. However, whether God saved them or not, they would not bow to the statue.
- Read Daniel 3:24-30. Recall the intense heat of the furnace (verse 22). Somehow Nebuchadnezzar was able to see into the furnace. He saw four men walking around, unbound and unaffected by the fire. According to Nebuchadnezzar, the fourth man looked like a "son of the gods." What was Nebuchadnezzar's reaction to what he saw in the furnance? How did Shadrach, Meshach, and Abednego experience God that day? What did they learn about God?
- Reflect on your own life. When you are obedient to God, He reveals more of His character, purposes, and ways to you. What has God revealed to you as you have been obedient to Him? How have you experienced Him?

Getting Ready

- Greet each child by name.
- Distribute *Experiencing God Kids Learner Guide* and pencils.
- Guide the children to complete "Crack the Code" (page 1).
- Invite the children to share their favorite foods.

Excite (5-8 MINUTES)

- Guide the children to complete "Is That Good for Me?" (page 2).
- Say: "We talked about some of our favorite foods. God has given us a lot of different types of foods to eat. Some of these foods are more healthy than others. Let's identify healthy and unhealthy foods."
- Call attention to the *Healthy* and *Unhealthy* signs.
- Distribute a food picture and tape strip to each child.
- Say: "Look at your food item. Decide how healthy or unhealthy you think the item is. Place it under *Healthy* if you think it is good for you. Place it under *Unhealthy* if it is bad for you. You can place the picture somewhere in the middle if you think it is both healthy and unhealthy."
- Guide the children to place their pictures.
- Call attention to the placement of the food pictures.
- Invite the children to state why they selected the placements.

Examine (10 MINUTES)

- Display the spaghetti or steak dinner.
- Ask: "Are you hungry? Would you like to eat this food?"
- Continue: "Or would you rather have this food?"
- Display the plate of fruits and vegetables.
- Allow the children to state which plate of food they would rather eat.
- Inquire: "How did you make a choice as to which food you would eat?"
- Serve the snack and water.
- Continue: "Imagine our country was taken over by another country. Some of you were taken to live in the other country. The king gave you his food to eat. Would you eat it? Why or why not?"

SUPPLIES AND PREP

Bibles, Session 8 *Experiencing God Kids Learner Guide* (1 per child), construction paper, markers, tape, magazine or food advertisements, scissors, spaghetti or steak dinner, plate of fruits and vegetables, fruit snack, water, cups, plates, napkins, pencils, "Reality 7" poster (Insert)

- Write *Healthy* and *Unhealthy* on 2 sheets of construction paper. Display on the focal wall about 5 feet apart.
- Cut food items from magazines or ads (at least 1 picture per child).
- Post an allergy chart listing all foods.
- Enlist someone to give a testimony of how she experienced God working in her life.

TIP

Provide exotic fruits such as star fruit, lychee, or dragon fruit.

LEADER GUIDE **SESSION 8**

Explore (25 MINUTES)

- Say: "Let me ask you a few questions. Tell me which one you would rather do."
- Ask: "Would you rather ride a roller coaster or watch someone ride one? Why?"
- Continue: "Would you rather watch a video of fireworks, or go to a park and watch live fireworks? Why?"
- Inquire: "Would you rather eat an ice cream cone or watch a friend eat it? Why?"
- State: "For most of us, we would rather experience something ourselves instead of watching a video, seeing pictures, or watching someone else do something. The experiences we have in life help us learn things. For example, if you have ever been near a fire, you know it is hot. You experienced the heat of the fire. If you forget to do your homework, you make a bad grade at school. If you drink lemonade, you know what it tastes like."
- Say: "Think about your most exciting experience. On the count of three, everyone, at the same time, shout out your experience."
- Count to three and allow the children to shout out their experiences.
- Continue: "Today we will discover how we can experience God and know Him better when we obey Him. Just reading about God and His commands in the Bible is not the same as believing and following them. When we trust God and obey Him, we experience Him for ourselves."
- Display the "Reality 7" poster.
- Select a volunteer to read aloud the poster.
- Ask: "Does this sound like the 'Crack the Code' message you discovered today?"
- Choose a volunteer to read aloud "Crack the Code."
- Say: "Listen carefully to our Bible story and discover how four young men experienced God working in their lives."
- Explain: "I need your help as I tell the story. I will tell you when to mimic my actions and repeat the words I say."
- Open your Bible to Daniel 1.
- Tell the Bible story in your own words.

CRACK THE CODE

I can learn more about God when He speaks to me and I obey Him and experience His power in my life.

A LIFE-CHANGING EXPERIENCE

Many years ago, the people of Israel disobeyed God. They stopped following Him and began to worship idols. God warned the people that if they continued to disobey Him, He would allow their enemies to capture them and take the people away. The people did not listen, and God did what He said He would do. King Nebuchadnezzar of Babylon invaded Israel and defeated the nation. He took many of their treasures and some of the people back to Babylon. Some of the young men taken to Babylon included Daniel, Hananiah, Mishael, and Azariah. This is their story.

[Establish a pattern of slapping your right knee, left knee, then clapping hands.]

> We're going off to Babylon, Babylon, Babylon
> We're going off to Babylon, but we're not afraid. *[kids echo phrases]*
>
> We've put our faith in God alone, God alone, God alone
> We've put our faith in God alone, and we're not afraid. *[kids echo phrases]*
>
> We've got our friends at our side, at our side, at our side
> We've got our friends at our side, and we're not afraid. *[kids echo phrases]*

Once Daniel, Hananiah, Mishael, and Azariah reached Babylon, things began to change. King Nebuchadnezzar changed their names. Daniel's new name was Belteshazzar (bel tih SHAZ uhr). Hananiah became Shadrach, Mishael became Meshach, and Azariah became known as Abednego. Even though the king gave the young men food from his own table to eat, Daniel decided not eat the king's food. He asked the guard to give him and his friends only vegetables and water for 10 days.

[Establish a pattern of slapping your right knee, left knee, then clapping hands.]

> There was lots of food to eat, food to eat, food to eat
> There was lots of food to eat, but we all said no. *[kids echo phrases]*
>
> Give us only vegetables, vegetables, vegetables
> Give us only vegetables, and water to drink. *[kids echo phrases]*
>
> Test us for the next 10 days, next 10 days, next 10 days
> Test us for the next 10 days, then check out our strength. *[kids echo phrases]*

The guard agreed to Daniel's request. At the end of 10 days, Daniel, Shadrach, Meshach, and Abednego looked healthier than the rest of the young men. God gave these four men the ability to know and understand the Babylonian literature and language. God gave Daniel the ability to understand all kinds of dreams.

Finally, the day arrived for the young men to be tested by the king.

[Establish a pattern of slapping your right knee, left knee, then clapping hands.]

It is time for our test, for our test, for our test
It is time for our test, to see what we have learned. *[kids echo phrases]*

The king talked with us, talked with us, talked with us
The king talked with us about what we learned. *[kids echo phrases]*

We answered all the questions, all the questions, all the questions
We answered all the questions and got the answers right. *[kids echo phrases]*

King Nebuchadnezzar was pleased with Daniel and his friends. In every area he questioned them, the men were 10 times smarter than anyone else in the kingdom.

Sometime later, King Nebuchadnezzar built a 90-foot high, golden image. He called all the leaders and people of his kingdom together. This is what he told the people.

[Establish a pattern of slapping your right knee, left knee, then clapping hands.]

This is what I command, I command, I command
This is what I command of every one of you. *[kids echo phrases]*

When you hear the trumpet sound, trumpet sound, trumpet sound
When you hear the trumpet sound, you will all bow down. *[kids echo phrases]*

If you do not bow, do not bow, do not bow
If you do not bow to the furnace you will go. *[kids echo phrases]*

King Nebuchadnezzar warned the people, "If you do not bow down and worship the statue, you will immediately be thrown into the fiery furnace."

As soon as the people heard the trumpet and other musical instruments sound, everyone bowed down and worshiped the statue. Everyone, that is, except Shadrach, Meshach, and Abednego. Some of the king's leaders reported to him that these three men did not bow down to the statue. The leaders told the king, "These men do not serve your gods. They don't worship the statue you made."

Extremely mad, King Nebuchadnezzar questioned the men; *[Establish a pattern of slapping your right knee, left knee, then clapping hands.]*

I want to know is it true, is it true, is it true
I want to know is it true, that you won't bow down! *[kids echo phrases]*

> When you hear the trumpet sound, trumpet sound, trumpet sound
> When you hear the trumpet sound, you will all bow down. *[kids echo phrases]*
>
> If you do not obey me, obey me, obey me
> If you do not obey me, the furnace you will see. *[kids echo phrases]*

The king warned the men one more time. Once again, the young men refused to bow to the statue. They said to the king, *[Establish a pattern of slapping your right knee, left knee, then clapping hands.]*

> We will worship God alone, God alone, God alone
> We will worship God alone, we won't bow down. *[kids echo phrases]*
>
> God will take care of us, care of us, care of us
> God will take care of us, this you will see. *[kids echo phrases]*
>
> In the furnace we will go, we will go, we will go
> In the furnace we will go, O great king. *[kids echo phrases]*

The king was so mad he ordered the furnace heated seven times hotter than normal. He commanded some of his strongest men to tie up Shadrach, Meshach, and Abednego. The fire was so hot the heat killed the soldiers who put Shadrach, Meshach, and Abednego into the furnace.

The king looked into the furnace and asked; *[Establish a pattern of slapping your right knee, left knee, then clapping hands.]*

> What is this that I see, that I see, that I see
> What is this that I see, four not three. *[kids echo phrase]*
>
> Why are there four men there, four men there, four men there
> Why are there four men there, walking in the fire? *[kids echo phrase]*
>
> One looks like a son of the gods, son of the gods, son of the gods
> One looks like a son of the gods, bring those men to me. *[kids echo phrase]*

Shadrach, Meshach, and Abednego were brought out of the furnace. The king's leaders crowded in around them. The leaders saw there was no damage to their clothes or bodies. The men did not even smell like smoke.

King Nebuchadnezzar said, *[Establish a pattern of slapping your right knee, left knee, then clapping hands.]*

> Praise to your God alone, God alone, God alone
> Praise to your God alone, He rescued you. *[kids echo phrase]*

LEADER GUIDE SESSION 8

REVIEW QUESTIONS
1. What was the name of the king who captured Israel? *(Nebuchadnezzar)*
2. What did Daniel ask for himself and his friends to eat? *(vegetables)*
3. How many days did Daniel ask the chief official to test him? *(10)*
4. How tall was the statue King Nebuchadnezzar had built? *(90 feet)*
5. What did Shadrach, Meshach, and Abednego refuse to do? *(bow to the statue)*
6. How many times hotter did Nebuchadnezzar have the furnace heated? *(7)*
7. When the king looked in the furnace, how many people did he see? *(4)*
8. What did the king say the fourth person in the furnace looked like? *(a son of the gods)*
9. What did King Nebuchadnezzar do after having the men brought out of the furnace? *(praised God)*
10. The first person to locate the balloon will name a way he has experienced God working in his life.

TIP
Assist the children in locating the verse.

These men trusted God, trusted God, trusted God,
These men trusted God, He protected them. *[kids echo phrase]*

These men risked their lives, risked their lives, risked their lives
These men risked their lives to serve their one true God. *[kids echo phrase]*

- Ask: "How do you think Daniel and his friends felt when they were taken off to Babylon? Why did king Nebuchadnezzar change their names and want them to learn about Babylon?"
- Explain: "Daniel and the other men had Hebrew names that referred to God. However, their new Babylonian names referred to Babylonian gods."
- Direct the children to complete "What's In a Name?" (page 6).
- Continue: "Why did Daniel and his friends not want to eat the food the king offered them? How did Daniel and his friends impress the king? How did the king reward them? When Nebuchadnezzar made the golden statue, what problem did Shadrach, Meshach, and Abednego face? What did they say to King Nebuchadnezzar that took a lot of faith and courage? What happened when they were thrown into the furnace?"
- Inquire: "Because Daniel and his friends were determined to obey God, even in a foreign land, what did God do for them? What did they learn about God? How did God use Daniel and his friends in Babylon?"
- Allow the children to respond.
- Inquire: "Have you ever been in a situation where you needed God to help you? What did you do? Have you ever had to take a stand for something you knew was right even if everyone else said you were wrong? How did it make you feel?"
- Say: "Let's discover how God used someone in our church in an amazing way."
- Invite the guest to share her testimony.
- Continue: "God wants each of us to experience Him every day. We may never face being thrown into a fiery furnace because we do not bow down to a statue, but we will face other challenges. When we do what God tells us, we can experience His power in our lives. Let's discover what Jesus said about experiencing God."
- Guide the children to locate John 14:23 in their Bibles.
- Select a volunteer to read aloud the verse.
- Direct the children to complete "Doing What Jesus Said" (page 8).
- Explain: "Jesus said God will come and live with us. When we ask Jesus to be our Savior and Lord, God lives in us. We call this the Holy Spirit. God, through the Holy Spirit, speaks to us and helps us obey Him and experience His power in our lives."
- Pray, thanking God for the Holy Spirit who helps each person learn about and experience God's power.

Engage (20 MINUTES)

ENGAGE OPTION ONE: FIERY FURNACE DIORAMA
- Guide each child to select a shoe box.
- Place the craft supplies on the table.
- Say: "Imagine your box is the furnace in our Bible story. Use the craft supplies to create a fiery furnace diorama (scene)."
- Assist as needed.
- Review the Bible story as the children design their dioramas.
- Ask: "How did Daniel, Shadrach, Meshach, and Abednego experience God working in their lives?"
- Continue: "How can we experience God working in our lives?"
- Share a personal testimony of God working in your life.
- Display the dioramas for parents to see.
- Invite the children to pray sentence prayers asking God to help them have the courage to obey Him and experience His working in their lives.

ENGAGE OPTION TWO: YES/NO QUESTIONS ONLY
- Form three teams.
- Display the box.
- Explain: "Inside the box is an item. One team at a time will ask yes/no questions related to the item in the box. I will only answer yes or no. As long as your team receives yes answers, you may continue asking questions. When I answer no, your team loses its turn and the next team begins. Listen carefully to all of the questions and answers. See if your team can be first to guess the item."
- Designate a team to begin.
- Answer yes/no questions until a team guesses the item.
- Award the item to the team to hold.
- Place another item in the box and continue as time permits.
- Display all of the items.
- Ask: "What do these items have in common?"
- Relate the items to the Bible story.
- Ask: "How did Daniel, Shadrach, Meshach, and Abednego experience God working in their lives?"
- Continue: "How can we experience God working in our lives?"
- Share a personal testimony of God working in your life.
- Invite the children to pray sentence prayers, asking God to help them have the courage to obey Him and experience His working in their lives.

SUPPLIES AND PREP
Shoe boxes (1 per child), clay, construction paper, scissors, glue, craft sticks, additional items to design diorama, table

TIP
Encourage the children to work together in groups.

SUPPLIES AND PREP
Shoe box with lid, items related to the Bible story (vegetable, bottle of water, small statue, trumpet, picture of fire, numbers 3 and 4)
- Place 1 item in the box and the other items out of sight.

TIPS
- Ensure the children understand the yes/no question format.
- Do not answer questions not asked in yes/no format.

LEADER GUIDE **SESSION 8**

SUPPLIES AND PREP

4 colors of inflated balloons, permanent marker, "Reality 7" poster (Insert), 3 laundry baskets, masking tape

- Write the words of "Reality 7" on the balloons (1 word per balloon, 1 set per team).
- Write the answers to the "Review Questions" (page 74) on the balloons. (Place to the side.)
- Tape a large circle on the floor.
- Place baskets on opposite ends of the playing area.

ENGAGE OPTION THREE: RACE TO THE FINISH

- Form three teams.
- Guide the children to stand around the outside of the taped circle.
- Guide the children to read aloud the "Reality 7" poster.
- Place the balloons in the circle.
- Assign each team a balloon color.
- Say: "Written on the balloons are the words of the seventh reality of experiencing God. When I say 'go,' one person from your team will enter the taped circle and locate one of your team's balloons. Without touching the balloon with any part of your body, get the balloon into your team's basket. Remember, you cannot touch any of the balloons with any part of your body. Once the balloon is in the basket, another member of your team will bring back another balloon. Continue until you get all of your team's balloons in your basket. Once all of the balloons are gathered, tape them to the wall in order of the seventh reality."
- Play the game.
- Place the answer balloons in the center of the playing area.
- Say: "This time, I will read aloud a question. The answer is written on one of the balloons. One person from your team must crawl to the center, locate the correct balloon and bring it back to your team. Only one correct answer is in the center, so work quickly to find the balloon. The team with the most balloons at the end of the game is the winning team."
- Select a player from each team to begin.
- Read aloud the first "Review Questions" (page 74) and allow the children to locate the correct balloon.
- Continue as time permits.
- Ask: "How did Daniel, Shadrach, Meshach, and Abednego experience God working in their lives?"
- Continue: "How can we experience God working in our lives?"
- Share a personal testimony of God working in your life.
- Invite the children to pray sentence prayers asking God to help them have the courage to obey Him and experience His working in their lives.

Ending The Lesson

- Display and review the realities of experiencing God.
- Ask: "What have you learned about experiencing God?"
- Invite the children to respond.
- Summarize and tie the realities of experiencing God together.
- Say: "God wants us to learn who He is, what He is doing, and for us to join Him in His work. He has special plans for us!"
- Call attention to "Experiencing God at Home" in the *Experiencing God Kids Learner Guide* (page 12).
- Challenge the children to complete the activities at home.
- Close the session in prayer.

SUPPLIES AND PREP

"Reality 1–7" posters (Insert)

WHAT HAS GOD DONE IN YOUR LIFE RECENTLY?

WERE YOU SURPRISED BY HIS WORK?

Session 9:
THE CHOICE IS MINE

Teacher Preparation

BIBLE PASSAGE
2 Kings 12:2; 23:25;
2 Chronicles 24; 34–35

BIBLE TRUTH
I can experience God working in my life.

LIFE APPLICATION
I can choose to be a part of God's plans for my life.

KEY VERSE
Hebrews 11:6

PRAYER CHALLENGE
Before beginning your planning, pray God will prepare your heart and work through you to speak to the children. Pray God will prepare the children to hear and apply what they learn so they can experience all He has planned for them.

- Read 2 Kings 11:21–12:19 and 2 Chronicles 24.
- Notice the background of Joash's (JOH ash, also called Jehoash, jih HOH ash) life. Joash's grandmother (daughter of King Ahab) attempted to kill all of Judah's royal family. At the age of seven, Joash became king. He lived under the influence and protection of his uncle, the priest Jehoiada (jih HOY uh duh).
- Reflect on the spiritual renewal Joash attempted to bring to Israel. Joash had the temple repaired and reestablished regular sacrifices and offerings. However, after Jehoiada's death, Joash began to listen to the counsel of other leaders. These men influenced him to turn from God and worship idols.
- Notice God's attempts to get Joash's attention. God sent prophets to speak, but Joash and the people would not listen. The prophet Zechariah (ZEK uh RIGH uh), Jehoiada's son, warned the people what would happen to them because they had forsaken God. Joash had Zechariah killed. Joash had become more concerned with the opinions and favor of the people than of God. Under Joash's reign, Israel suffered at the hands of the Syrians. Ultimately, Joash was assassinated by his own servants.
- Read 2 Kings 22–23 and 2 Chronicles 34–35.
- Compare the lives of Joash and Josiah (joh SIGH uh). At the age of eight, Josiah became king. Even as a young boy, Josiah sought God. As a teenager, he set out to remove the idols and practice of idol worship from Judah. In the process of the temple repairs, the Book of Law was discovered. Hilkiah (hil KIGH uh), the high priest, brought the book to Josiah. How did Josiah respond when he heard the Book of Law read? Why was Josiah to be spared from experiencing the judgment that was to befall Israel?
- Notice Josiah's concern. He had the Book of Law read before the people. He led the people to renew their covenant to follow God. Josiah continued his efforts to cleanse the land of all idolatry and occult practices. He reinstated the observance of Passover.
- Reread 2 Kings 23:25. How was the life of Josiah summarized? Josiah believed God and made changes to obey and experience God's blessings. God used him to turn some, not all of the people back to God.

- Think about your own life. Are you more like Joash or Josiah? In what ways? Are you choosing to be a part of God's plan for your life? Pray for guidance and direction as you help children understand how they can be a part of God's plan.

Getting Ready

- Greet each child by name.
- Distribute *Experiencing God Kids Learner Guide* and pencils.
- Guide the children to complete "Crack the Code" (page 1).
- Invite the children to talk about choices they made during the last week.

SUPPLIES AND PREP
Bibles, Session 9 *Experiencing God Kid's Learner Guide* (1 per child); scissors, "Reality 1-7" posters (Insert), 2 toy crowns, construction paper, marker, tape, pencils
- Copy "Reality 1–7" posters and cut into jigsaw puzzle shapes.
- Write the life application statement on a piece of construction paper.

Excite (5-8 MINUTES)

- Say: "Over the last eight weeks we discovered seven realities to experiencing God. Let's see if you remember each of the statements."
- Guide the children to complete "Test Your Memory" (page 2).
- Say: "Let's put some puzzles together and check our answers."
- Place the puzzle pieces on the floor.
- Invite the children to work together to assemble the puzzles.
- Read aloud and review each reality statement. Allow the children to correct any mistakes on their "Test Your Memory" (page 2). Ask questions related to the Bible stories about each of the realities.

Examine (10 MINUTES)

- Display the crowns.
- Select two children and place the crowns on their heads.
- Ask: "If you were selected to be the king of a country, what are some things you would do? Would you make any new laws? Would you do away with any laws? What would you tell the people about God?"
- Invite the children to respond.
- Say: "Today we will learn about two of the kings of Israel. One of the men became king at the age of seven. The other was only eight when he became king."
- Continue: "Girls, open your Bibles to the Book of 2 Kings. Boys, locate 2 Chronicles in your Bibles."
- Assist as needed.
- State: "The Books of 1 and 2 Kings and 1 and 2 Chronicles tell the stories of the kings of Israel and Judah. When we read all four of the books, we can learn more about these rulers. We can also learn which ones followed God and which ones did not. Today we will learn about Joash and Josiah. Girls, listen for some things these two kings had in common. Boys, listen for the differences in these men."

TIP
Provide poster board and markers. Allow the kids to list differences and similarities as you tell the Bible story.

Explore (25 MINUTES)

- Open your Bible to 2 Chronicles 24.
- Tell the Bible story in your own words.

TWO YOUNG KINGS, TWO DIFFERENT DECISIONS

Joash was only seven years old when his father, King Ahaziah (ay huh ZIGH uh) of Judah, died. At the age of seven, Joash became king of Judah. Joash's uncle, Jehoiada (jih HOY uh duh) was the priest. During Jehoiada's lifetime, Joash did what was right and followed God's plans. At some point in his reign, Joash decided to repair the temple, the place where the people worshiped God. Joash gathered all of the priests and Levites together and instructed them, "Go throughout all of Judah and collect the taxes people owe. We will use the money to repair the temple." The Levites did not listen to Joash.

Joash asked his uncle, Jehoiada, "Why have you not instructed the Levites to gather the money?" Joash commanded a chest be placed at the temple gate. He issued an order that stated all the people in Judah and Jerusalem were to bring their taxes and place them in the chest. All the people gladly brought the money they owed and placed it in the chest. Joash and Jehoiada gave the money to the workers to repair the temple. Once the temple was completed, the people worshiped God. As long as Jehoiada was living, the people followed God. At the age of 130, Jehoiada died.

Following the death of his uncle and priest, Joash began to listen to the suggestions of other people. The people stopped going to the temple. They even began to worship false gods. God became angry with Joash and the people. God sent prophets to speak to the people, but they would not listen. One man, Zechariah (ZEK uh RIGH uh, Jehoiada's son) stood before the people and said, "God asks, 'Why do you disobey My commands?' Because you have turned away from God, He has turned away from you." The people did not like what Zechariah said. King Joash gave permission and Zechariah was stoned to death. Joash even had Jehoiada's sons (Joash's cousins) killed.

Shortly after the new year began, the army of Aram (AHR uhm) fought against Joash and his army. All the leaders of Joash's army were killed. Joash himself was badly wounded. The officials of Joash's army were upset that he had killed Jehoiada's sons, so they killed Joash.

- Open your Bible to 2 Chronicles 34.

Following the death of his father King Amon, Josiah became king at the age of eight. He ruled Jerusalem for 31 years, always trying to follow God's plans.

At the age of 16, Josiah began to seek God. Josiah wanted to know what God wanted him to do. At the age of 18, Josiah began to remove all the idols and items used to worship false gods from Jerusalem and Judah. Altars were destroyed and other images and false gods were removed. At the age of 26, Josiah repaired the temple dedicated to the worship of God.

While the workers were repairing the temple, Hilkiah (hil KIGH uh), the high priest, found the Book of Law. The Book of Law was a scroll containing the things God had spoken to Moses. Hilkiah gave the book to a man named Shaphan (SHAY fan), the king's secretary. Shaphan read the book to Josiah. Josiah was very upset when he heard the words of the Book of Law. He knew the people were not obeying God. Josiah sent some of his men to learn what would happen to the people because of their disobedience. Hilkiah and the other men went to the prophetess Huldah (HUHL duh). Huldah told the men, "God will punish the people for their disobedience. Everything the Book of Law says will come true because the people have turned away from God. However, because King Josiah has humbled himself, repented of his sins, and knows the sins of the people, God will not punish the people until after Josiah's death."

After hearing what Huldah said, Josiah gathered all the leaders and people of Judah and Jerusalem together. He and all the people went to the temple. Josiah read aloud the Book of Law to the people. Josiah publically renewed his promise to follow God and obey His commands. He led all the people to promise to do the same. As long as Josiah lived, the people followed God.

Josiah led the people to once again observe the Passover festival (a special celebration to help the people remember how God saved them from Egyptian slavery).

In a battle with Neco (NEE koh), king of Egypt, Josiah was badly wounded. He died and was buried in Jerusalem. All the people of Judah and Jerusalem mourned for him.

- Ask the girls, "In what ways were Joash and Josiah alike?"
- Ask the boys, "In what was were Joash and Josiah different?"
- Compare and contrast the men's lives.
- Continue: "Which king followed God's plan for his life? How do you know God was at work in these men's lives? Which king loved God and wanted a relationship with Him? How did God speak to King Joash? Did Joash listen? How did God speak to King Josiah? How did God use King Josiah? What did the people and Josiah learn about God? Which king helped his people?"
- Say: "We may not be kings or rulers, but God wants to use us, too. He loves us and wants a personal relationship with us. God is working all around us. We can all be a part of His plans."

CRACK THE CODE
I can choose to be a part of God's amazing plan.

- Ask: "What message did you discover in 'Crack the Code'?"
- Select a volunteer to read aloud the "Crack the Code" answer.
- Display and read aloud the life application poster.
- Ask: "What are some of the key words of this sentence?"
- Underline the word *I*.
- Say: "Each of us must make an individual choice to be a part of God's plan. Even though I would like to make the choice for you, you must make the decision yourself."
- Underline the word *choose*.
- Continue: "We must choose to be a part of God's plan. God will not force us to do anything. He wants us to freely decide to follow Him."
- Underline the words *for my life*.
- Explain: "God has a plan for everyone. The plans He has for me are not the same as the plans He has for you. God has plans for each of our lives."

LEARNING TO PLEASE GOD
Without faith it is impossible to please God.

- Ask: "What does it take to please God?"
- Guide the children to complete "Learning to Please God" (pages 6-7).
- Select a volunteer to read aloud the completed statement.
- Direct the children to locate Hebrews 11:6 in their Bibles.
- Choose a volunteer to read aloud the verse.
- Say: "Without faith, we cannot please God. We have learned a lot of information about a lot of different people. Look at 'People Who Experienced God' (pages 4-5). Each of these people experienced God in a unique way. Each person had faith that God was working in his life. Just as God worked in these people's lives, God is working in our lives. God wants us to have faith and choose to follow Him."

TIP
Offer to talk with children individually about their feelings on following God.

- Ask: "What is something all of these people had in common?"
- Allow the children to state commonalities.
- Continue: "Every one of these people had to make changes in their lives. Some had to be willing to move to different places. Some had to change their jobs. Others had to change what they believed about God. When we choose to follow God's plans for our lives, we have to be willing to make changes. Following God is an exciting adventure."
- Guide the children to bow their heads and close their eyes.
- Say: "Some of you may be excited to join God in His plans. Others of you may be scared about what God will do in your life. Take time to tell God how you feel."
- Pause for silent prayer.
- Close the prayer time thanking God for His plans regarding each person's life.

Engage (20 MINUTES)

ENGAGE OPTION ONE: FAITH BRACELETS
- Say: "Have you ever thought about the fact that for every choice you make there is a consequence? A consequence could be good or bad."
- Ask: "What were some of the choices Joash and Josiah faced? What consequences did they face?"
- Say: "Let's make bracelets to remind us to have faith to please God."
- Distribute beads and lacing.
- Explain: "On one end of the lacing, tie a knot about 3-inches from the end."
- Assist as needed.
- Continue: "Place three beads on the string, sliding them as close to the knot as possible. Then place the *f, a, i, t,* and *h* beads on the string. Next, place three more beads on the string and tie a knot as close to the beads as possible."
- Assist as needed.
- Guide: "Ask a friend to help you tie your bracelet on your arm. Trim off the extra lacing."
- Ask: "What is faith? Why is faith important?"
- Say: "*Faith* is 'belief that what God has told a person about Himself is true.' We can have faith that God has plans for our lives. When we trust what He said is true, we can choose to follow His plans and be a part of His work."
- Invite the children to make additional bracelets to share with their friends.
- Explain: "When you see your bracelet, remind yourself to choose to follow God's plans for your life. If someone asks you about your bracelet, tell her how you learned to experience God working in your life."
- Pray, thanking God for the ways He is working in and through the lives of the children.

SUPPLIES AND PREP
Pony beads (variety of colors, including ones with *f, a, i, t, h* letters) at least 1 set per child, craft lacing or thick yarn, scissors, ruler
- Cut lacing into 15-inch strips (at least 1 per child).

ENGAGE OPTION TWO: FIND THE ANSWERS
- Say: "Have you ever thought about the fact that for every choice you make there is a consequence? A consequence could be good or bad."
- Ask: "What were some of the choices Joash and Josiah faced? What consequences did they face?"
- Guide the children to form two teams and line up at the opposite end of the room from the cards.
- Say: "Our game will help us review everything we learned about experiencing God. One person from your team will be the 'king.' He will place the crown on his head. I will read aloud a question. The 'kings' will run and find the card from his team's cards with the correct answer. The first 'king' to bring back the correct card earns 1,000 points for his 'kingdom.' Let's see which 'kingdom' can earn the most points."
- Select two children to be the "kings."
- Read aloud the first question (pages 84-85).
- Allow the "kings" to race to locate the correct answer cards.

SUPPLIES AND PREP
2 toy crowns, scissors
- Print and cut apart 2 sets of "Answers" (page 89).
- Mix all the cards together. Randomly place the cards at the opposite end of the playing area.

TIP
Copy "Answers" on different colored paper for each team.

LEADER GUIDE SESSION 9

TIP
Ask the children to recall some of their favorite "Engage" activities from the study. Replay the activities as time permits.

1. According to Jeremiah 29:13, God tells us that we will find Him when we do what? Need a clue?—When you look for something, you are searching for it. *(search for Him with all our heart)*
2. What is God always doing around us? Need a clue?—Most adult do this to earn money. *(work)*
3. We learned about a lot of different people seeking God and following His example. This person is the perfect example of being a part of God's work. Need a clue?—He is God's Son. *(Jesus)*
4. When the King of Syria was at war with Israel, he thought there was a spy in his camp. No spy was present. God was telling this man about the king's plans. Need a clue?—The man's name starts with the fifth letter of the alphabet. *(Elisha)*
5. Deuteronomy 31:8 says God will never do what? Need a clue?—Read the verse in your Bible. *(leave you)*
6. What can we learn from Elisha's servant? Need a clue?—Two words in the answer are *recognize* and *work*. *(God will help us to recognize Him at work around us.)*
7. What did Jesus do when He saw the disciples sending the children away? Need a clue?—Look for the word *children*. *(rebuked the disciples and told them to let the children come to Him)*
8. According to John 3:16, God loves the world. Who is the world? Need a clue?—It is me, you, and all people. *(everyone)*
9. We learned that God wants this kind of "ship" with us. Need a clue?—It is not a rocket ship or spaceship. *(relationship)*
10. Jesus used a young boy's lunch to feed over 5,000 people. What did the boy have for lunch? Need a clue?—The numbers two and five are important. *(2 fish and 5 loaves)*
11. According to Ephesians 2:10, God has prepared something for us to do. What is it? Need a clue?—The first word is the opposite of bad. *(good works)*
12. Samuel thought he heard Eli call him; however, it was not Eli. Who was calling Samuel? Need a clue?—He is calling you to join Him in His work. *(God)*
13. According to Jeremiah 29:11, who knows the plans for our lives? Need a clue?—He knows everything. *(God)*
14. God speaks to us in different ways. Find a card with four of these ways listed. Need a clue?—Look for the cards with numbered answers. *(1. Bible, 2. prayer, 3. circumstances, 4. church)*
15. According to Hebrews 11:6, without this it is impossible to please God. Need a clue?—Read Hebrews 11:6 in your Bible. *(faith)*
16. What must we be willing to do in our lives in order to follow God's plan? Need a clue?—Things cannot always remain the same. *(change)*
17. Shadrach, Meshach, and Abednego refused to bow to the golden image. As a result, they were thrown into one of these. Need a clue?—It can get really hot in there. *(furnace)*
18. When we obey and follow God, two things happen. What are they? Need a clue?—You KNOW the answer. *(experience God more and get to know Him better)*

19. Does God hide His purpose for our lives from us? You do not need a clue. *(No)*
20. No answer card is available for this statement. As a group, name three things you learned about experiencing God. *(Answers will vary.)*

- Verify the answer and award points.
- Select new "kings" and continue the game.
- Say: "We learned a lot about experiencing God. The challenge for us now is to apply what we learned. God wants us to be a part of the work He is doing. He has plans for every one of us. Let's choose to join Him."
- Pray, thanking God for the way He is working in and through the lives of the children.

ENGAGE OPTION THREE: USING THE BIBLE

- Say: "We learned a lot about experiencing God. The challenge for us now is to apply what we learned. God wants us to be a part of the work He is doing. He has plans for every one of us. As we continue reading and studying the Bible, we will learn more about being a part of God's work. Let's use our Bibles to play a game. I will ask you a question about one of the books of the Bible. When your team has found the answer, shout 'Got It!' The first team to find the answer earns 1,000 points, the second team 750, the third team 500."
- Form three teams.
- Read aloud the questions one at a time. Award points and continue as time permits.
  » Genesis is the first book of the Bible. How many chapters are in the Book of Genesis? *(50)*
  » Exodus 2 tells about the birth of whom? *(Moses)*
  » Psalm 119 is the longest chapter in the Bible. How many verses does Psalm 119 contain? *(176)*
  » What is the last word in the Bible? *(Amen)*
  » According to Mark 1:9, what was name of the river in which Jesus was baptized and who baptized Him? *(Jordan, John the Baptist)*
  » John 2:1-11 tells about Jesus' first miracle. What was it? *(turning water to wine)*
  » According to Acts 14:8-12, in what city were Paul and Barnabas worshiped as gods? *(Lystra)*
  » Zechariach 1:8 tells about the prophet Zechariah having a vision of a man riding a red horse and standing under what kind of tree? *(myrtle)*
  » Matthew 4:18-22 tells about Jesus calling the first disciples. Who were the first two men chosen as disciples? *(Andrew, Simon Peter)*
  » According to John 11:1, in what town did Mary and Martha live? *(Bethany)*
  » According to Proverbs 22:1, what is to be desired more than great riches? *(a good name)*
  » Which book comes after the Book of Galatians? *(Ephesians)*
  » According to Psalm 56:3, when you are afraid, what should you do? *(trust in God)*
  » According to 1 John 4:7, what should we do? *(love one another)*
  » What is the last book of the Old Testament? *(Malachi)*

SUPPLIES AND PREP
Bibles, paper, marker, tape
- Secure the paper to the wall for keeping score.

- Say: "By reading and studying our Bibles we learn how to live in ways that please and honor God."
- Challenge the children to read and study their Bibles every day.
- Pray, thanking God for the way He is working in and through the lives of the children.

Ending The Lesson

- Say: "Let's celebrate that God loves us and has plans for our lives."
- Serve the snack items.
- Display and review the realities of experiencing God.
- Ask: "What did you learn about experiencing God?"
- Invite the children to respond.
- Continue: "How does it make you feel to know God wants you to join Him in His work?"
- Summarize and tie the realities of experiencing God together.
- Challenge the children to complete the remaining activities in their booklets at home.
- Complete and sign each child's certificate (page 12).
- Close the session in prayer.

SUPPLIES AND PREP
Cupcakes, juice boxes, napkins, other party foods and supplies, "Reality 1-7" posters (Insert)

- Prepare and post an allergy alert chart.
- Create a celebration atmosphere.

TIPS

- Read aloud *Sammy Experiences God* (ISBN 1433679809). Review the 7 Realities of Experiencing God and connect them to Sammy's life.
- Provide each child a copy of *Sammy Experiences God* to take home.

WHAT DID GOD DO THROUGH YOUR LIFE AS A RESULT OF THIS STUDY?

WHAT DID GOD DO THROUGH THE LIVES OF THE CHILDREN?

search for Him with all our heart	work
Jesus	Elisha
leave you	God will help us to recognize Him at work around us.
Rebuked the disciples and told them to let the children come to Him	everyone
relationship	2 fish and 5 loaves
good works	God
God	1. Bible, 2. prayer, 3. circumstances, 4. church
faith	change
furnace	experience God more and get to know Him better
No	

LEADER GUIDE **ANSWERS**

SESSION 1

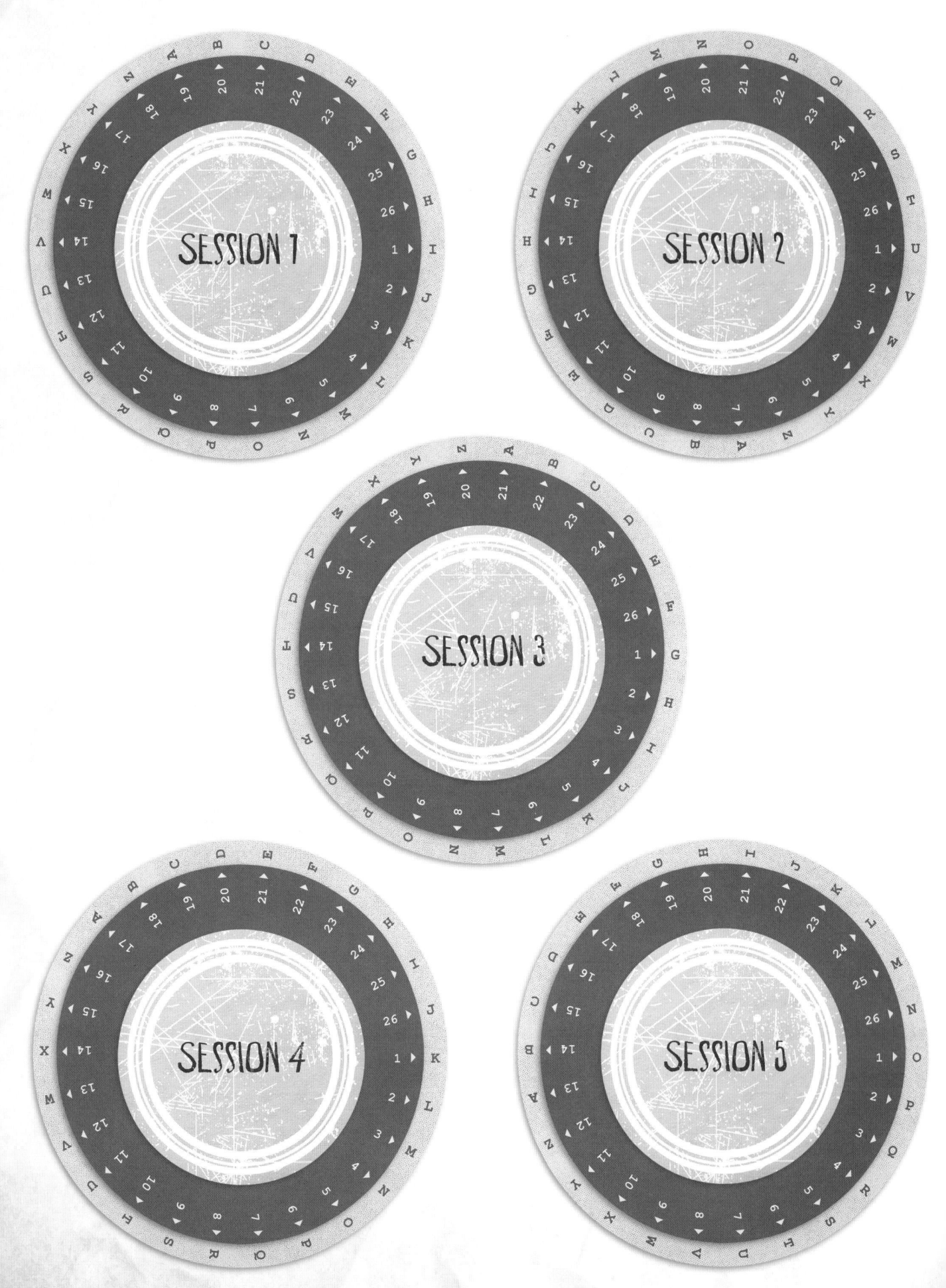

SESSION 2

SESSION 3

SESSION 4

SESSION 5

EXPERIENCING GOD AT HOME **KIDS**

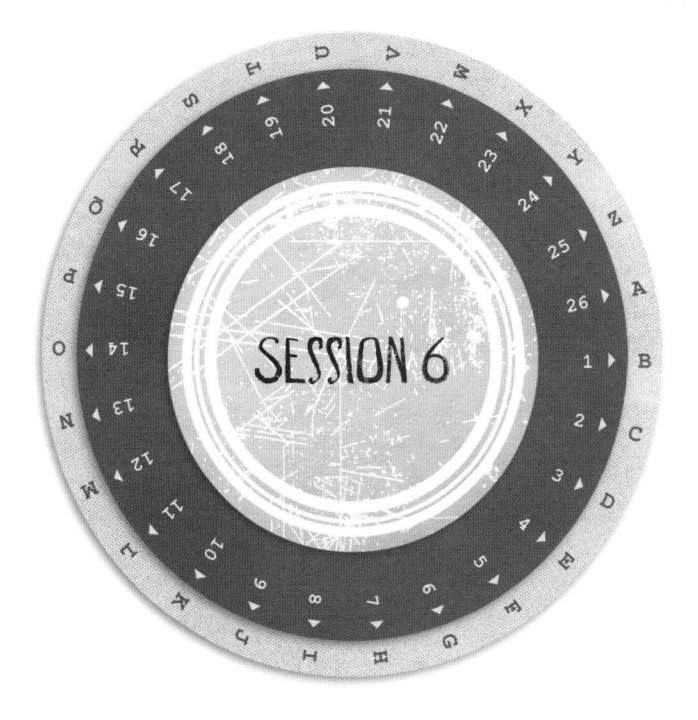

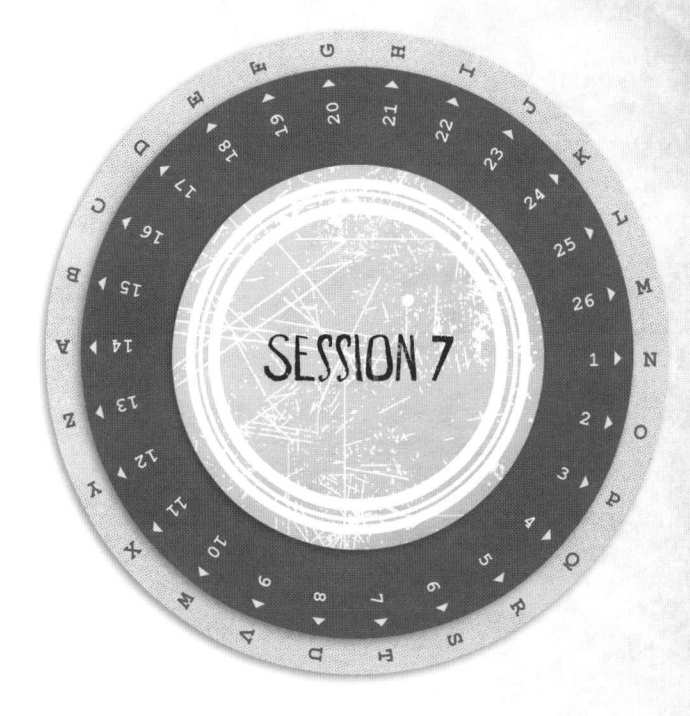

SESSION 1: I will learn how God is working in my life.

SESSION 2: I can ask God to show me where He is at work around me and how I can be involved in what He is doing.

SESSION 3: I can know God loves me and wants a relationship with me.

SESSION 4: I can learn to recognize when God is inviting me to be a part of what He is doing.

SESSION 5: I can learn to understand when God is speaking to me.

SESSION 6: I must have faith and take action to follow God and join in His work.

SESSION 7: I must be willing to change my attitudes and actions to follow God's plan.

SESSION 8: I can learn more about God when He speaks to me and I obey Him and experience His power in my life.

SESSION 9: I can choose to be a part of God's amazing plan.

LEADER GUIDE DECODERS

THE LONELY KING

will be able to talk with me whenever he pleases." The king looked down at Johnny, "I hope you'll come."

"Sure! Can my mommy come too?" Johnny asked.

"Sure" the king responded smiling. He squeezed Johnny's hand and looked up to continue, "Let it also be known in all my kingdom that from this day forward if anyone wants to talk with me, he or she needs to become like this bold little boy. He wasn't afraid to talk with me, welcome me in, be real with me, and accept me as a personal and caring king. All those who follow his example, I will receive openly, hear freely, and answer enthusiastically.

As the king began to walk back with Michael, the crowd at first began to part to let them through. Then slowly, one person after another approached the king and spoke to him like he was a real person. By the time the king reached his palace gate, his pace had slowed to a crawl because person after person came to shake his hand and speak to him. The king was overjoyed. From that day forward, everyone began to follow Johnny's example.

That night, the king stopped to look out of his crystal walls toward King's Park. He smiled when he noticed something that others may not have noticed. Every garbage can between his palace and the park was filled to overflowing with crumpled pieces of paper.

Once upon a time, in a large, peaceful and powerful kingdom that encompassed majestic mountain ranges, lush green valleys, powerful rivers, beautiful land that seemed without end and millions of always-smiling subjects, there lived a great king. Many said he was the greatest king who ever was and would ever be. In fact, he was so wise and powerful that people didn't even call him by his name. He was simply and respectfully called "The King". The king's castle was so big that it had the largest city ever built inside its walls. It was said that the castle was so huge that if you stood outside the walls and looked straight up on a clear day you couldn't see the top. If you rode the fastest, strongest horse in the kingdom and never stopped—day or night, it would take you three months to just ride around the city one time.

The castle's spectacular gates were always open and the king was always busy. He met with and talked to thousands of people every day. It was a big kingdom after all. The king had servants, assistants, politicians, and personnel of all sorts. But he, of course wanted to oversee everything because he loved his people dearly and wanted their lives to work well. He met and talked and planned with every one of his helpers. He not only talked with all of those who helped him run a perfect kingdom, but he also talked with the hundreds of

"Are you my king?" the boy asked, hugging the king's neck.

"Yes, I am," the king answered hugging him back. "What's your name?"

"I'm Johnny," said the boy peering out from under his mussed up hair. "Why are you at the park?" Johnny asked.

"I was hoping to talk with someone just like you," the king replied. "Is everything in your life OK? Is there anything that a king could help you with?" the king asked.

"I'm happy. My mom says I'm a bit bold, though. It's probably because I like to talk with people a lot," Johnny said.

"Me too!" the king said wiping something from His eye. "I guess that makes us both bold" the king said laughing.

If it was someone's job to put their hands on other people's chins and gently close their mouths when their mouths were hanging open in astonishment, that person would be working for a year to close the mouths of this crowd. The king stood up and took Johnny by the hand. Then he spoke to the people. It has been said that every single subject in the entire kingdom heard the king's voice that day. "From this day forward, this boy will be to me as a son and I will be to him as a father. He will be allowed to come and go freely in my presence and

his subjects who came to see him every day. Some people came to ask him for help, for favors, for wisdom, or for justice. Many came to ask for things (because everyone knew that the king was the richest king who ever was and that he was extremely generous to all).

At the end of each long day, the king would walk slowly through his amazing castle toward his beautiful and luxurious private quarters. He barely noticed the gold covered floors, the crystal clear walls that let him see the beauty of his kingdom, the art made from jewels set in the walls or even the impressive guards with their gleaming armor who would bow as he passed. All he could think about was how lonely he was. Now you might very well ask, "How can a person who is so great and who is loved by millions and who talks to more people every day than perhaps anyone else be even a little lonely?" That would be a good question; a question that the king thought about often. Here was the problem: perhaps lonely wasn't the right word. The king was so great that people were nervous and acted awkward in front of him. Most people just read from a piece of paper or even a book when they talked to him. Some of the people memorized statements and they would just repeat the same words to him every day, day after day. Whenever the king would try to get someone to just talk to him like he was a real person, the people just stood still, not knowing what to say. The king felt so bad for the people that he

As the king looked away from Michael's eyes, he looked down the road. Thousands of his subjects were following, wondering what was happening. The king looked around. There were crowds coming down every street—the word was spreading the king was in the park. The king smiled a BIG smile and waved. Everything was going according to plan. Michael followed closely as the king walked to the largest playing field in the park. He made his way to the top of a grassy hill in the center where some children were playing. He stood at the top, watching the kids as thousands crowded onto the field and up the hill toward him. When everyone stopped, the king sat down on the grass in the middle of the group of small children. A very large chorus of small gasps escaped from the people and then King's Park went absolutely silent. Michael could hear the silence spread out. Within a minute, it seemed like the word had spread and with it the silence, until the entire kingdom had gone silent. Suddenly, one of the children laughed and jumped on the king. The silence was broken with a second gasp that seemed to travel like a wave. The king held up his hand and all went silent again. A little boy looked around, then looked back at the king.

allowed them use what they had written or memorized.

As the king reached his private quarters he thought, "I'm not lonely; I just wish people would let me into their hearts." Then he had an idea.

"I want to go into the town tomorrow, Michael," the king said to the head of his guard, walking just behind him.

"Yes, your Majesty. I'll arrange your royal carriage, the trumpeters, your personal guard and ..."

"No, all that won't be needed," the king interrupted, "I'll walk on my own. However, you can come with me if you'd like to walk with me."

"Yes ... Your Majesty ..." replied Michael, not knowing what else to say.

The next day the king, dressed in comfortable walking clothes, strolled with Michael down the streets of the kingdom. People were shocked to see him and didn't know what to do. Some bowed deeply, others who had talked to the king before fumbled through their pockets looking for their pieces of paper. The king waved, smiled, and kept on walking. An hour later, Michael started looking nervous. He had no idea where the king was going.

"We're almost there Michael," the king said pointing down the street. Michael looked confused. The king was pointing to King's Park. It was perhaps the most beautiful and spacious park in the kingdom, but everyone knew it was the place where the children played.

Michael started to make plans in his head trying to think through what he could do to prevent the kids from climbing all over the king—that just wouldn't be right! These kids hadn't seen the king before and probably didn't know how to behave properly. Then a disturbing thought struck Michael, *What if the kids said something wrong or disrespectful to the king!? They had probably never been taught to talk properly to the king!*

At the edge of the park the king stopped, turned, and looked Michael right in the eye.

"You look nervous, Michael," the king said with a smile, "Whatever happens I don't want you to interfere with myself and the children. Do you understand?"

Michael gulped and nodded "Yes, your Majesty."

SITUATION 1: My name is Elizabeth. I am 10 years old. I could really use your help. Gerald, a kid in my class, said some pretty mean things about Samantha. Samantha overheard Gerald and she is really upset. She is crying. What can I do to help Samantha? Should I say something to Gerald? If so, what should I say?

SITUATION 2: My name is Keith. I am nine years old. I could really use your help. Some kids in my neighborhood were talking about a movie they watched. The movie mentioned Jesus and the Bible. Based on what the movie said about Jesus, the kids have some strange ideas about Him. I don't believe what they said about Jesus. I think the movie said many things about Jesus that are not true. What should I do? Should I say something to them? What if they tell me I don't know what I am saying?

SITUATION 3: My name is Denise. I am seven years old. Gillian is a girl in my class. She has been sick a lot lately. Her parents took her to the doctor. The doctor said Gillian has cancer. I'm not sure what cancer is, but it does not sound like something I want. Should I go visit Gillian? What can I say to help her?

LEADER GUIDE **SITUATIONS**

HOW GOD SPOKE ... Amber's teacher was planning a party for the class. She challenged the kids to pray about who God wanted them to invite to the party. Amber hoped to invite some children who do not come to church and might not know about Jesus. Amber asked God who she should invite. As she prayed, she thought of Melanie. Amber did not know Melanie very well and was a little shy to invite her to the party. The next day in school, Amber was surprised when she and Melanie were paired up for a math activity. As they worked on the activity, Amber asked Melanie if she would like to go to the party. Melanie said her family did not attend church, but she had always wondered what people did there. She would love to go.

HOW GOD SPOKE ... Vanessa could not believe it was her first day of fourth grade! She had been placed in Mrs. Foster's class, but none of her close friends were in her class! Vanessa was so upset. She asked her mom to call the principal and see if she could be placed in a different class. Vanessa prayed God would make it happen. The principal said it would not be possible to change classes. Vanessa wondered why God did not answer her prayer. Without her usual friends, Vanessa began to spend time with Katy. Katy was so shy and Vanessa had never really noticed her before. The two girls sat next to each other and always seemed to be placed in the same work groups. As they got to know one another, Katy began to ask Vanessa about God and the Bible. Katy began to go to church with Vanessa's family and later that year, Katy became a Christian.

HOW GOD SPOKE ... Adam became a Christian at summer camp last year. Lately, he had thought about getting baptized, but he was not sure. In his Bible study class, Adam learned about John the Baptist baptizing Jesus. In worship, the pastor announced a baptismal service was being scheduled in two weeks. Adam's teacher asked him if he had any questions about baptism, or about being baptized. God seemed to be telling Adam something.

HOW GOD SPOKE ... Monica was supposed to sing a solo at school tomorrow. She was really nervous. She had never sung in front of that many people. What if she could not do it? The night before, Monica began to read in her devotional book. The Scripture verse was Philippians 4:13. *[Read aloud Philippians 4:13.]* God reminded Monica she could do it because He would help her.

HOW GOD SPOKE ... Trey's family went on a mission trip to Haiti. While they were there, they worked in an orphanage. When Trey's family saw how many children needed a loving home, they started to think about adopting a child. Trey's family already had three children. Did God want them to adopt a child? Trey's family began to pray. Every day they asked God to help them know what they should do. They talked with their pastor and other Christian friends who had adopted. Trey's family started to feel this was what God wanted them to do. On the day they drove to the adoption agency to begin the adoption process, Trey's mom turned on a Christian radio station. The radio announcer was reading James 1:27. *[Read aloud James 1:27.]* Trey's parents looked at each other and smiled.

LEADER GUIDE **HOW GOD SPOKE**

Home Connection

Parents,

Your child is beginning an amazing adventure. During the next several weeks we will explore seven realities of *Experiencing God* and how these realities relate to your child's life. We will discover God has a plan for each person, how to join God in His plan, as well as the changes we must make to follow God's plan. Here are some things you can do to assist your child in learning to experience God.

- Arrive on time. Each week we will begin on time. Please make sure your child is present.

- Ask questions. During the session, your child will discover how God worked in the lives of a Bible person. Ask your child to tell you what he discovered and how it applies to his life.

- Encourage your child to complete the "Experiencing God at Home" activities (page 12 of the learner booklets).

- Look for ways God is working in your child's life and comment on the actions you observe.

- Share your personal testimony of what God is doing in your life.

- Pray for and with your child on a daily basis.

These are just a few suggestions of ways you can help your child learn to experience God working in his life. Please know the teachers are taking their jobs very serious. We will seek to work alongside God as He works in your child's life. If we can assist you in any way, please do not hesitate to let us know.

1. Had a skin disease *(Naaman)*

2. Taken captive and had to serve Naaman's wife *(servant girl)*

3. Told Naaman to go to Elisha, a prophet in Samaria *(servant girl)*

4. Told the king of Aram what the servant girl said for him to do *(Naaman)*

5. Told Naaman to do what the servant girl said *(king of Aram)*

6. Gave Naaman a letter to take to the king of Israel *(king of Aram)*

7. Sent a letter to the king of Israel telling Naaman to come to him *(Elisha)*

8. Told Naaman to wash himself seven times in the Jordan River *(Elisha)*

9. Was upset Elisha did not come and touch him and heal him *(Naaman)*

10. Learned there is only one God *(Naaman)*

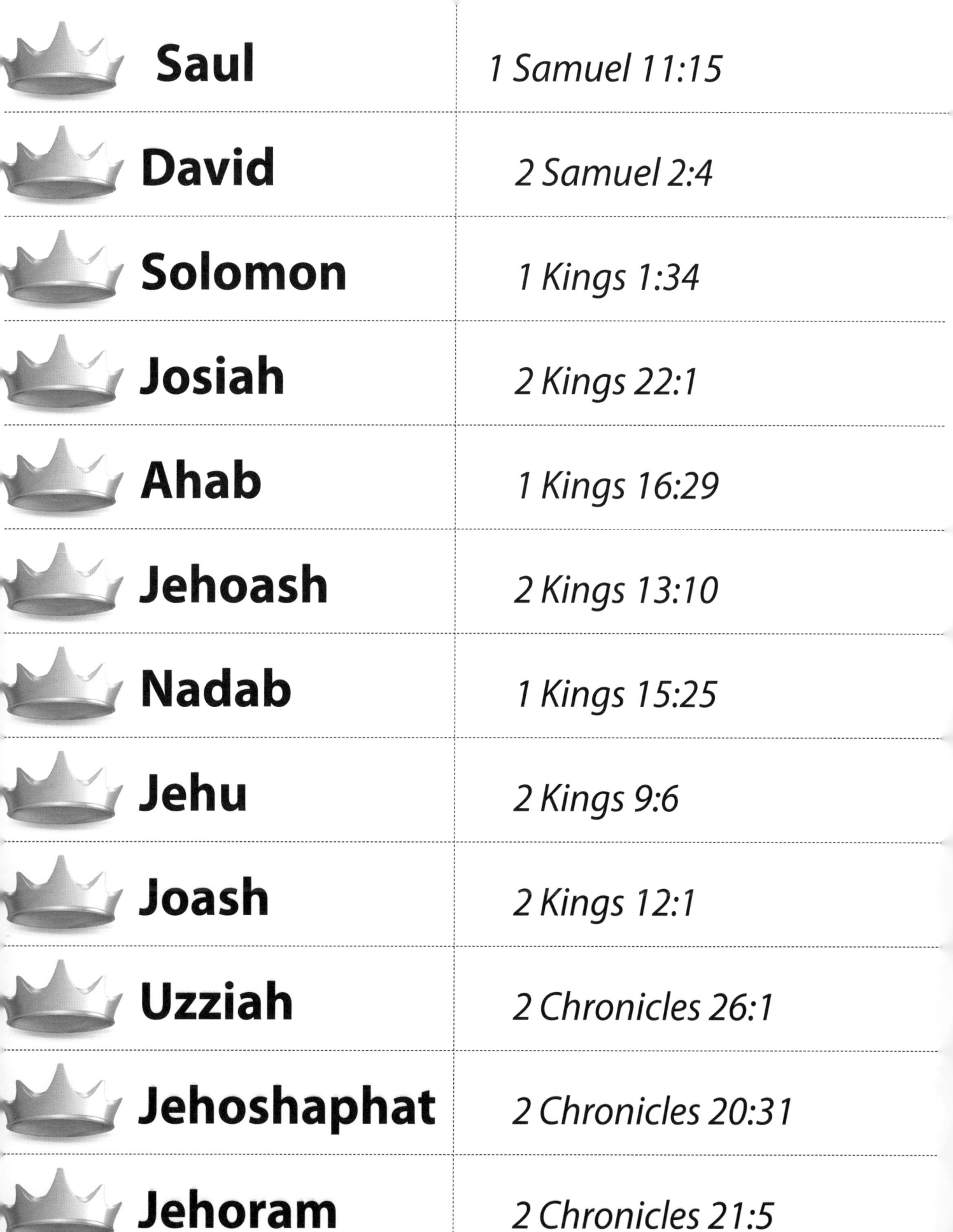

👑	**Saul**	*1 Samuel 11:15*
👑	**David**	*2 Samuel 2:4*
👑	**Solomon**	*1 Kings 1:34*
👑	**Josiah**	*2 Kings 22:1*
👑	**Ahab**	*1 Kings 16:29*
👑	**Jehoash**	*2 Kings 13:10*
👑	**Nadab**	*1 Kings 15:25*
👑	**Jehu**	*2 Kings 9:6*
👑	**Joash**	*2 Kings 12:1*
👑	**Uzziah**	*2 Chronicles 26:1*
👑	**Jehoshaphat**	*2 Chronicles 20:31*
👑	**Jehoram**	*2 Chronicles 21:5*

LEADER GUIDE **KINGS**

Pray
Philippians 4:6

Trust
Proverbs 3:5-6

Listen
Job 42:4

Wait
Psalm 27:14

Watch
Isaiah 41:20

Check
1 Thessalonians 5:21

LEADER GUIDE **REMINDERS**

Follow Instructions

1. Carefully read all of the instructions before beginning.
2. Say out loud, "I love doing silly things!"
3. Give someone a gentle hug.
4. Hop up and down three times on one leg.
5. Tell someone the name of one of your pets (if you have one).
6. Snap your fingers.
7. Smile the biggest smile that you can smile.
8. Quote a Bible verse to a teacher.
9. Sing a line from your favorite song.
10. Stand up and twirl around.
11. Say something nice to a teacher.
12. Pretend you are playing a musical instrument.
13. Clap your hands together 10 times.
14. Say your whole name out loud.
15. Say this tongue twister four times quickly: Silly Sammy Simkin simply smiled.
16. Find something to write with and draw a happy face on your paper.
17. Yawn and stretch.
18. Whistle or hum the song "Jesus Loves Me."
19. Stand up and say a nursery rhyme.
20. Find something blue in the classroom and go touch it.
21. Ask yourself, "Did I follow the first instructions?" If not, go back and read them.
22. Stand at attention and salute.
23. Pat yourself on the back.
24. Check to see if anyone in your class is seated quietly with his arms folded.
25. Do not follow any of the instructions on this sheet from 2 to 24—only follow 1 and 25. Congratulations, you're finished! Just sit with your arms folded without talking so the teacher will know you are finished.

Home Connection

The *Kids Experiencing God at Home* materials are designed for church use; however, the hope is parents will continue the learning experiences in their homes. The kids learner booklets include an "Experiencing God at Home" page (page 12 of the booklets). This page includes a checklist of activities for the children to complete. Call attention to the page and recommend the children complete the page with their parents. Here are some other activities you can do to encourage the parents to continue the learning experience at home.

- Provide a parent meeting/training time before beginning the *Experiencing God* Bible study. Overview the sessions and what the children will discover each week. Talk with parents about how they can continue the learning throughout the week.

- E-mail parents following each session. Review the biblical content, *Experiencing God* reality, life application, and a few questions to talk about with their children.

- Call families throughout the study to offer assistance. Ask how the study is making a difference in the lives of their children.

- Copy "Home Connection" (page 108) and distribute to parents.

- Pray for each family on a daily basis.

- Encourage the children to bring their completed *Experiencing God* booklets back each week. Provide treats for the children who complete all of the activities.

LEADER GUIDE HOME CONNECTION